THE HEART
OF GOD
for her

45 Day Devotional Revealing God's
Love for His Leading Ladies

A Compilation by
Allison Denise Arnett

TABLE OF CONTENTS

DEDICATION

To every woman and girl.
Arm in arm, we grow stronger together.

ACKNOWLEDGMENTS

Thank You Holy Spirit for the divine inspiration for this devotional.

Thank you to each of the writers who thought it not robbery to bravely share their stories to lift another woman up.

Thank you to my team who helped me put this together so beautifully.

FOREWORD
— Roshanda E. Pratt —

THERE IS A mantra I get to share with women that I support globally in their journey in life and business: "Visibility is Power." The reality is, for many women being seen and heard seems foreign and almost unobtainable. There is an internal battle between the voice that God has given us and the whispers of the enemy. We remain silent with little to no impact or we succumb to the pressure. There is an identity issue that has been in place since the creation of man and woman. Scripture likens the woman to wisdom and her worth, far above rubies. However, from Biblical times to the present, the constant fight for understanding the heart of God for His daughters continues to rage like a wildfire out of control.

God loves creation especially those created in His image and likeness. When God created the wild animals each according to their kind, God saw that it was good. When God created mankind in His own image, He blessed them and called them very good. Daughter, you are very good and blessed by your Father. I realize this may seem strange, but in the natural world, you may not have been blessed and called good by a biological father or another man figure in your life. However, God is ready to have an encounter with you to reveal His heart to you, His beloved daughter.

So, the question remains, why don't more women understand the heart of God towards them, their value in His eyes, and their impact in the world? After all, it was the influence of Eve's decision, which caused Adam to stumble from the beginning of creation. Visibility is power gives us some insight in that we must understand the heartbeat of God for His beloved. John 15:9, "As the Father has loved me, so have I loved you. Now remain in my love."

For the next chapters, you are diving into a journey of

revealing the Heart of God for you. After reading these transparent, transformational stories of real-life women and their parallel stories with women in the Bible, you will feel both inspired and motivated to draw closer for a deeper relationship with God. This beautifully written piece of work features stories from women pouring from their alabaster box to confidently and passionately serve God with all their hearts. Now is the time to get to the heart of the matter-- You are the heart of the matter.

Roshanda E. Pratt
Storyteller, Live Stream Strategist & First Lady of Visibility
www.therosholive.com
IG/FB: @TheRosholive

DAY 1

God Has Better for You!
(Abigail)
— Robin Cuffee-King —

"And when the servants of David were come to Abigail to Carmel, they spake unto her, saying, 'David sent us unto thee, to take thee to him to wife'.
– 1 Samuel 25: 40

ABIGAIL WAS KNOWN for her beauty, discretion, grace, and wisdom. Nabal, her husband was an evil and cruel man with lots of money who was often given to drunkenness. You could say that Abigail was forced to be in a toxic relationship by being married to this man.

As time went on, Nabal would make a decision to shear some of his own sheep. This caught the attention of David who had been protecting Nabal's, sheep, and servants from any possible harm. David felt that Nabal should know about the protection he provided for his servants. David was hoping that Nabal would be generous in return and give him and his men some of the sheep so they could eat. This would turn out to be a blessing in disguise. And David heard in the wilderness that Nabal did shear his sheep. "And David sent out ten young men, and David said unto the young men, Get you up to Carmel, and go to Nabal, and greet him in my name: And thus shall ye say to him that liveth in prosperity, Peace be both to thee, and peace be to thine house, and peace be unto all that thou hast. And now I have heard that thou hast shearers: now thy shepherds which were with us, we hurt them not, neither was there ought missing unto them, all the while they were in Carmel. Ask thy young men, and they will shew thee. Wherefore let the young men find favour in thine eyes: for we come in a good day: give, I pray thee, whatsoever cometh to thine hand unto thy servants, and to thy son David." (1 Samuel 25: 5-8)

When Nabal had received the words of David from the young men who had been sent, he responded with an insult. "And Nabal answered David's servants, and said, Who is David? and who is the son of Jesse? there be many servants nowadays that break away every man from his master.11 Shall I then take my bread, and my water, and my flesh that I have killed for my shearers, and give it unto men, whom I know not whence they be?" (1 Samuel 25: 10-11)

One of the young men that served Abigail and Nabal was aware of the words that his master had spoken against David. He decided that he would inform Abigail of what had occurred before David returned with hundreds of his men to cause bloodshed. The young man pleaded with Abigail letting her know that her husband and all that they owned were in trouble. "But one of the young men told Abigail, Nabal's wife, saying, 'Behold, David sent messengers out of the wilderness to salute our master; and he railed on them. But the men were very good unto us, and we were not hurt, neither missed we anything, as long as we were conversant with them, when we were in the fields. They were a wall unto us both by night and day, all the while we were with them keeping the sheep. Now, therefore, know and consider what thou wilt do; for evil is determined against our master, and against all his household: for he is such a son of Belial, that a man cannot speak to him. (1 Samuel 25:14-16)

Abigail knew that it was just a matter of time before these men would show up and destroy all that she knew because of her husband's unsavory ways. So, she took time to get together some items that would serve to appease David and his men, and show them they were valued and respected.

Abigail's actions caused David's heart to be changed. He

decided that he would adhere to her request and not cause any bloodshed. Can you believe that when Abigail told her husband Nabal what she had done the next morning his heart was hardened? Ten days later, God smote him and he died.

David, after the news reached him that Nabal had died, saw an opportunity to take Abigail as his wife and Abigail agreed. "And when the servants of David were come to Abigail to Carmel, they spake unto her, saying, 'David sent us unto thee, to take thee to him to wife'. And she arose, and bowed herself on her face to the earth, and said, 'Behold, let thine handmaid be a servant to wash the feet of the servants of my lord'. And Abigail hasted, and arose and rode upon an ass, with five damsels of hers that went after her; and she went after the messengers of David, and became his wife." (1 Samuel 25: 40-42)

Beyond any relationship; beyond any shortfalls, I believe that God has greater for you. While Abigail's story shares insight on the struggles of a toxic relationship, I know we have all been there. We have been in toxic relationships and even stayed in places that we knew no longer served us. Beyond those moments, when we are finally able to break free we then began to see that God had a greater plan for us.

My sister, I truly believe that for anytime that you have felt like you have been forced to settle God provided a way of escape into something better. Even if you find you are currently struggling with what seems to be good but truly isn't, I am praying for a swift escape to the greater that God has for you.

Pray this prayer with me
Father, we need you like never before. Heal us from any brokenness and toxic place in our life. Whether it be a relationship or something else, God we know that You can free us from it all. May we grow in the knowledge of who You have called us to be so that we know that we do not have to accept

anything less than the abundance You have planned for us. In Jesus name, amen.

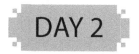

DAY 2

Age ain't Nothing but a Number
(Anna the Prophetess)
— Patti Denise Henry —

"And there was a prophetess, Anna, the daughter of Phanuel, of the tribe of Asher. She was advanced in years, having lived with her husband seven years from when she was a virgin, and then as a widow until she was eighty-four."
– Luke 2:36-38

THE STORY OF Anna the Prophetess is found nestled in the gospel of Luke, Chapter 2, Verses 22-38. There was nothing said of her before or after. Her story began when Jesus, as a child, was taken into the city of Jerusalem to the temple by his mother and father to be presented to God as a symbol of purification, which was customary in that day.

Anna, after being married for only seven years, became a widow. After the death of her husband, she lived a life of sacrifice and faithfulness in the House of God. Anna spent her days worshipping God in the temple. Anna was a prophetic intercessor which was a unique position for a woman to hold in that day. What is even more unique is that instead of remarrying after her husband died, Anna chose as a very young woman to remain a widow and serve God in the temple. I imagine that as people came to make their offerings to God they sought her counsel. They trusted her wisdom and revelatory words.

Scriptures reveal that Anna was 84 years old when Mary and

Joseph entered the temple with Jesus. Anna was led by the Spirit of God and recognized who Jesus was. After giving thanks, she bravely declared to his parents and all who were listening that Jesus was the one for whom they were waiting. She told them that he was the one that would redeem the people of God. His parents marveled at what she had said.

Like Anna, many aging adult women are anointed, full of power, and in tune with the revealed will of God for future situations. I am in Chapter 57 of my life book. I have wrestled with the thought of getting older. I questioned my effectiveness for God. The Holy Spirit whispered to me one day and let me know that it took 57 years to prepare me for my assignment! I felt assured that God wasn't finished with me yet. My heart is forever open to all that is possible.

Many people will try to disqualify you because of your gender and your age. You may be counting yourself out or creating yet another method to sabotage God's plan and destined purpose for your life. You may have experienced grief, singleness, or slowed down because of age. It is no accident that you were drawn to this book. God's plan for you will be fulfilled because He has a heart for you and knew who you were when He created you. You may have more years behind you than you have ahead of you but believe me, when I tell you this, your best days are ahead.

Affirmation: Psalm 138:8 "The Lord will work out His plan for my life and because of His loving-kindness, He will never abandon me."

Pray this prayer with me:

Father, I approach you with confidence because of all that your son, Jesus Christ, has done for me. I have experienced a myriad of obstacles which led me to believe that I had nothing left to give. I believe and accept that all of your promises are yes and amen. You keep your word. Your word never returns until it completes the tasks it was assigned. Thank you for seeing me, and for creating me with a purpose and a plan. Thank you for having a heart for me and for perfecting all the things that concern me. Amen.

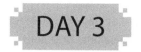

DAY 3

Follow God, Even If No One Else Does
(Athaliah)
— Brittaney Pleasant —

"Ahaziah also followed the evil example of King Ahab's family, for his mother encouraged him in doing wrong. He did what was evil in the Lord's sight, just as Ahab's family had done. They even became his advisers after the death of his father, and they led him to ruin."

– 2 Chronicles 22:3-4

AS WOMEN, ONE of the most beautiful things many of us get to experience is the joy of motherhood. From seeing and feeling our babies grow within our womb, to going through the process of birthing them; and finally getting to hold them in our arms as we welcome them into the world; to nurturing and guiding them into adulthood. While there are many things to enjoy about being a mother, the role does come with a lot of responsibility. It is our job to instill the right morals and values in our children to help them live a life that is pleasing to God. What happens when we don't receive those things from our parents? Are we left to figure things out for ourselves?

The story of Athaliah teaches a great lesson about this. Athaliah was the daughter of Ahab and Jezebel, who both worshipped idols. Athaliah followed in her parent's footsteps; she chose to worship Baal, even turning to murder to get her way. In spite of her upbringing, she still had a choice. God desires to have a relationship with all of His children so much that He will send people into our lives to help us establish or develop a closer relationship with Him. Such was the case for Athaliah. God sent her a godly man named Jehoram to be her husband. This could have been a turning point for Athaliah but instead of turning from the wicked ways and practices of her parents, she continued to follow and worship idols. She even influenced her husband to abandon his godly ways and turn to idol worship as well. This ultimately led to their untimely deaths.

Sometimes, we don't receive the nurturing guidance that we desire. We don't all grow up in homes where God's love is always exhibited. However, we should strive to be alert and aware of when God is speaking to us, and when He is calling us into a relationship with Him and trying to show us a better way to live. Sis, no matter what you have been through, how you were raised, or what you may have experienced or seen, know that God is always desiring to be close to you. Even if your mother or father did not know God, or simply chose not to follow Him, the story does not have to be the same for you. God desires to have a close relationship with you. He desires to know you, to guide you and to love you. Perhaps Athaliah did not have the courage to follow God after she witnessed her parents living a completely different lifestyle. Sometimes, we have to choose to follow God even if no one else does. Although it can seem scary, I assure you, having a relationship with Him is one of the best decisions you could ever make for your life and the lives of those around you. There is no greater love than the love of God and He desires to give it to you unconditionally.

Pray this prayer with me:
Dear Heavenly Father, I come before you asking you to show me that You desire a relationship with me. Show me that You loved me so much that while we were sinners, You sent Your only son to die for us. Let me know that I am worthy of Your love and that there is nothing that can separate me from the love You have for me. Give me the courage to deny myself, pick up my cross, and follow You so that I may experience the abundant life You have for me. In Jesus name, Amen.

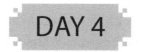

DAY 4

Mystery, Murder and Mercy
(Bathsheba)
— Deborah Rivers Decoteau —

He saw a woman washing herself; and the woman was
very beautiful to look upon.
– 2 Samuel 11:2

THE STORY OF Bathsheba found in 2 Samuel 11, is very intriguing.
It's springtime in Jerusalem. Most men, including her husband, were
on the battlefield.

Bathsheba decides to take advantage of the situation and
bathe outside. Unknown to her, King David was not on the battlefield
with the rest of his men. In fact, he was relaxing on his balcony when
he saw her. He was immediately captivated by her beauty. He sent
his messengers to inquire about her and even after learning that
she was the wife of Uriah, one of his best soldiers he continued his
pursuit. According to the bible, David was a man after God's own
heart. He knew better but did that deter him from satisfying his
own selfish desires? Of course not! He summoned her, she obeyed,
they slept together, she became pregnant. "Each one is tempted by
his own evil desire, then he sins and then sin gives birth to death."
James 1:14.

David was a powerful and wise king who had a weakness for
beautiful women. After committing the sin of adultery, and lying

about it, he had Bathsheba's husband, Uriah, killed in battle adding murder to his list of sins. Proverbs 15:3 says "The eyes of the Lord are everywhere, beholding the evil and the good". Bathsheba becomes David's wife and a baby boy is born.

An all-seeing, hearing, and knowing God did not let these horrible acts go unpunished. Despite David's desperate pleas for GOD's mercy to save his son's life, his son would die at the hand of God as punishment for David's sins.

I know we can all relate to this story in one way or another. Acting without thinking. As women we sometimes fall into that category because of our situations. Bathsheba had to have known her actions were wrong. She could have resisted David's advancements, but she did not. Maybe she was scared to say no to such a powerful man. Maybe she wanted him. No one really knows. In my life, I have had to repent and ask for forgiveness numerous times and each time my GOD was faithful, but not without chastisement. "God chastises those he loves" Hebrews 12:6. That is how I know he loves me, and he loves you too. Do not let fear cripple you in asking for forgiveness when you sin. Jesus paid the price for our sins in full at the cross over 2,000 years ago.

Do you have any unconfessed sins in your life? Confess your sins and repent. "He is faithful and just to forgive us our sins and cleanse us from all unrighteousness." 1 John 1:9. If you find yourself in a situation where your flesh wants to go against your faith you must stand on the promises GOD. Do not open the door to the devil; resist him, and he will flee. James 4:7.

How important do you think David and Bathsheba must have been to God? Very important. He showed them mercy and blessed them with another son, Solomon, whom God loved, 2 Samuel 12:24. "His mercies never end, they are new every morning" Lamentations 3:22-23. Bathsheba was used by God in the genealogy of Jesus because she was the mother of Solomon. God had a place in his heart for her, and he has one in his heart for you. GOD IS LOVE.

Pray this prayer with me:
Heavenly Father, thank You for looking out for the needs of women like me. Thank You for restoration and including me in Your plans. Remind me of your new mercies every morning. Amen

DAY 5

Bonus Blessings of a Willing Vessel
(Bithiah, Adoptive Mother of Moses)
— Monique M. Moorer and Natalie A. Bryan —

"Then Pharaoh's daughter went down to the Nile to bathe, and her attendants were walking along the riverbank. She saw the basket among the reeds and sent her female slave to get it. She opened it and saw the baby. He was crying, and she felt sorry for him".
– (Exodus 2:6-6a)

SOMETIMES, THE BLESSINGS we encounter are disguised. They can come from various avenues. But one place that you would not usually see it come from is your subordinate. That is where God's hand usually plays a major role. We can have our life planned out one moment, and then find ourselves going in a completely different direction. We could think that we have it all together but suddenly realize that we are in need of something and did not even know it. The Egyptian princess, Bithiah, was the daughter of the Pharaoh. She possessed status and clout. As a member of the royal household, she could have anything she wanted. What could she possibly want or need? She found a baby floating in a basket on the Nile river after her father sent out a decree to kill all the Hebrew boys. She raised this child as her own and named him Moses. Bithiah had compassion in her heart for Moses. Her endeavor to save him was rewarded. When Moses led the children of Israel out of Egypt, he saved Bithiah also. She was converted and left Egypt with the people of Israel. Upon leaving Egypt, she married Mered of the tribe of Judah and was blessed to enter into the promised land. "You shall treat the stranger who sojourns with you as the native among you, and you shall love him as yourself, for you were strangers in the land of Egypt: I am the Lord your God". (Leviticus 19: 33-34). Bithiah may have grown up believing that her days would begin and end in Egypt, but God had another plan for her.

God has a big blessing with you in mind. Sometimes, it is difficult to go against the grain; but doing so sets you apart from everyone else. There was a time during our school days that my sister Natalie and I, did not fit into our environment. We were scholars in school, yet social loners. Do not get me wrong, we were social butterflies. There were associates around that would smile and joke with us, but very few people really knew who we were. No matter how we were treated by others we always had a heart to give. A calling to put others' needs before our own. We were the self-sacrificial sisters that always adopted the underdog. We truly believe it is because that is how we felt about ourselves. We at least had each other. But everyone was not so fortunate to have supportive siblings. We seem to just find those people that were "left behind" and love on them. In doing so, God had blessings in store for us. One blessing was moving to a new state where strangers became family and success became apparent. Like Bithiah, we adapted well to our new surroundings, to our promised land. God did the rest. Blessings upon blessings have filled our homes and our hearts. Our blessings are not just of material things, but of favor.

Sometimes when you feel like you do not fit in the environment into which you were born, it may just be that God has called you to something different; something greater. Jeremiah 29:11 (NLT) says "for I know the plans I have for you," declares the LORD, "plans to prosper you and not to harm you, plans to give you hope and a future". When you trust the Lord and not your surroundings or your own thoughts God will raise you up before nations. As a Licensed Clinical Social Worker (LCSW) and in ministry, Natalie has helped people understand that they are not alone and that God is present in every circumstance. God is our refuge and our strength, an ever-present help in times of trouble. (Psalms 46:1 GWT). She has conveyed this message on the local news and social media. As a Licensed Practical Nurse (LPN), I Monique have and continue to assist doctors and patients for over twenty-one years. I am also a psalmist that ushers in the presence of the Lord in song during church services.

We both could have only dreamed of doing the things we are doing today, but God has pushed us through obstacles and opposition to get where we are. Like Bithiah, He wants you to do the same; be different. You are destined for greatness. Just step out of your comfort zone and out of your own way. Let Him work in you! That is what the Scriptures mean when they say, "no eye has seen, no ear has heard, and no mind has imagined what God has prepared for those who love him". (1 Corinthians 2:9 NLT). You will be amazed at what God can do with a willing vessel. You have got this!

Pray this prayer with me:

Thank You, Lord, for the protective angels that you have encamped over my life. As a woman who would sacrifice everything for someone she loves; as the mother of Moses gave up her child to save his life in Exodus 2:3, You have Sacrificed your only begotten son to save my soul. As I live in Your grace each day, I remember Your promise of everlasting life. I know that You have called me for something different. I know that you have put greatness in me. Your word says, "to whom much is given, from him much will be required" (Luke 12:48 NKJV). I am thankful for Your love. As You, God, used Bithiah to pull Moses from the water, Lord use me. I thank you Lord for any pivot and redirection You may cause is my life. I thank You for the destiny that You have pre-ordained just for me. Thank You, Lord, that you have given me the strength to step out of my comfort zone and to launch boldly in your name. I pray that the day I stand before you I hear you say "well done". I thank You and honor You in Jesus' name. Amen.

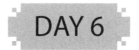

DAY 6

You are worthy of God's vision. Yes, you!
(Story of Deborah)
— Brejette Terry-Emery —

"For still the vision awaits its appointed time, it hastens to the end
it will not lie. If it seems slow, wait for it; it will surely come. It will
not delay."
– Habakkuk 2:3

DEBORAH WAS THE wife of Lapidoth; she was also a prophet and a
judge. She was leading Israel when the nation had fallen captive to
King Jabin of Canaan. The Israelites called on the Lord for help after
20 years of oppression. The Israelites went to Deborah for help with
their disputes.

Deborah sent for Barak son of Abinoam. Deborah told Barak
that the Lord wanted him to take ten thousand men to battle
against King Jabin's commander, Sisera. Barak stated he would only
go if she went with him. She stated she would go, but, the honor
of the victory would not be his. Not only that, but Sisera would
be defeated by a woman. Deborah went with Barak and things
happened just as she had prophesied. Sisera was taken in and killed
by Jael, wife of Herber.

Just like Deborah, we as women in business often find
ourselves filling multiple roles. We are wives, mothers, daughters,
sisters, and aunts. We are CEO's and leaders in the business world,
as well as leaders in the spiritual world. We often fill these roles out
of a nurturing spirit. The pressures to fulfill God's calling in our lives

causes us to challenge the ways of this world and its oppressive ways. I am reminded of the scripture "speak up for those who cannot speak for themselves, for the rights of all who are destitute. Speak up and judge fairly; defend the rights of the poor and needy." 1 Proverbs 31:8-9 We have to rise to the occasion and lead in times that we would rather blend in and not be seen.

Deborah was a unique woman. She was unique because she judged and led an entire nation. For all intents and purposes, she was a queen with a prophetic word for the nation of Israel. In Deborah's obedience to the Lord; she was able to confidently instruct Barak not only to go into battle but to also inform him of how the victory would be won. Yes, she would go to the battle with him and the Israelite army, but this was a battle he must fight. She would not be pressured to do his work, but she would stand with them and see the vision come to fruition.

As a spiritual, African American entrepreneur in the world, I often find myself forced to choose between being a woman, an African American, and a child of God. I have found it unacceptable to the world to be all at once. When I think about Deborah, she was able to stand firm and declare unapologetically that she worked for the Lord. "But seek first his kingdom and his righteousness, and all these things will be given to you as well. Therefore, do not worry about tomorrow, for tomorrow will worry about itself. Each day has enough trouble of its own." Matthew 6:33-34. When we are called, we do not have to choose between being a woman, a minority, or a child of God. We are free to be all that God has created us to be with pride. We can be confident in declaring God's grace and mercy on our lives. God's business is the business of saving lives and souls while spreading love, peace, and joy.

When Deborah spoke to Barak she did so without fear or question. I feel that I too often care what others think when God commands me to do things that others may not understand or approve. But God does not need the world's approval to do His will, and neither do we. Worrying about others' thoughts and opinions on your life will cripple your ability to go the distance. Had Deborah not followed God's instruction with such confidence and resilience, the Israelites would not have been freed. As women in power, we have to unite and rise to every occasion no matter the worldly distractions or deterrents, for we know that our God will not allow us to fail. We are reminded that "the thief comes only to steal and kill and destroy, I have come that they may have life, and have it to the full." John 10:10. Do not allow this world to rob you of God's calling on your life.

God loved Deborah so much that he gifted her leadership, authority, and prophecy over his people to lead them to freedom. Never doubt your ability to fulfill God's calling on your life for He has equipped you with everything that you need to complete the mission. Obedience, discernment, and vision are God's way of leading you through the chaos and confusion of this world.

Pray this prayer with me:
I ask You God, my Master, Jesus Christ, the God of glory to make me intelligent and discerning in knowing you personally, my eyes focused and clear so that I can see exactly what it is You are calling me to do. Lord, I humble myself and choose to keep my eyes focused on You, Your will, and Your way. Lord Jesus, make the vision plain. (Ephesians 1:17-18) Amen

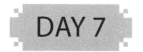

DAY 7

It Is Time to Get Up
(Dorcas (Tabitha))
— Robin Cuffee-King —

Peter made everyone leave the room. He knelt and prayed. Then he turned toward the body and said, "Tabitha, get up!" Tabitha opened her eyes, saw Peter, and sat up. Peter took her hand and helped her stand up. After he called the believers, especially the widows, he presented Tabitha to them. She was alive. The news about this spread throughout the city of Joppa, and as a result, many people believed in the Lord.
– (Acts 9:40-42)

TABITHA, WHOSE NAME is Dorcas in Greek, was a woman known for her generosity and supportive acts. She would sew garments for others and give to those who were in need. Many don't know, however, that she was also discipled by Jesus. If you search the New Testament you will find that the feminine form of the word disciple in Greek was only used once, and it was for her.

In the scripture text, we see that Tabitha died. Even though it seemed all hope was lost God said NO. When Peter came in, he carried with him a faith in Jesus so strong, that Dorcas had no choice but to obey the apostle and RISE up.

As a disciple of Jesus, Tabitha was taught how to live a life of giving. The way she cared for others and made sure that those in need did not go without, speaks to the power of what she was taught which ultimately impacted her ministry of service to others. While she is only mentioned once in the New Testament, her raising from the dead by the apostle caused many people to turn to Christ.

This story may seem ordinary but I assure you that it is relevant to a woman like you and me. We each strive to live and give. We help those who are needy and we pray that the light of God shines through any of our shortcomings. While you may not be laying on your deathbed, I believe that when we fail to give our full selves to the calling of God, we draw away from the fullness of life that He has for us.

I can remember the days when I refused to walk in the fullness that God had for me. I avoided accountability and made so many excuses as to why I could not obey. But then a change happened. I realized I could no longer make excuses. I had to change. I had a "Robin, get up!" moment with God, and if you are reading this, I hear God saying GET UP! You know that God has placed something on your heart to do. It calls out to you. Don't worry; that is simply the purpose God has for you.

So, are you ready to get up from what is deadening your purpose? God is calling out to your heart because He loves you. There are others who need what you have. Whether it be a garment or a resource what you have to offer is needed for those whom God has positioned to receive from you.

Pray this prayer with me:
Father, right now I pray that there will be a tug at my heart to do what You are purposing me to do. Let me hear You clearly and even when I am unclear on every detail, God, show me that as I respond to You with faith You will order my steps. In Jesus name, amen.

DAY 8

The Mother of a Miracle Child? Who, me?
(Elizabeth)
— Brejette Terry Emery —

"Do not be afraid Zechariah: your prayer has been heard. Your wife Elizabeth will bear you a son, and you are to call him John."
– Luke 1:13 NIV

ZECHARIAH, THE HUSBAND of Elizabeth, was visited by the angel Gabriel. He was told that his wife would be blessed with a son and the couple would have to name him John. Zechariah questioned the angel Gabriel and was struck mute until after the birth of the baby because he questioned the word of God. Elizabeth gave birth to a miracle baby boy, and in obedience named him John. John would later be called John, the Baptist and would be known as the forerunner for Jesus. Elizabeth's promise was fulfilled although she and her husband were old and she was barren.

I knew almost from conception that I had been blessed with a child. I did not have confirmation from any doctor or test but I knew in my spirit it was my turn. I had raised so many and helped raise so many. It was finally my time.

I was feeling under the weather and was dehydrated so I went to the doctor. She asked if there was any way that I could be with child. I stated it was possible since my husband (at the time) and I were no longer using protection. The doctor decided to do a pregnancy test which came back a false positive. Although the test was not positive I was filled with excitement as I believe Elizabeth to be. Unlike Zechariah's response in which he questioned being able to have children, I had no doubt. I can envision the doubters, and even family members that may have mocked Elizabeth, but God. Later, I received confirmation from the doctor that the blood test came back positive, confirming what I knew all along. Little did I know that would be the easiest of appointments to come.

In the first set of appointments, I was told the fetus was not growing at a normal rate, and I would have to see a specialist. At the next appointment, I was informed that the fetus's head was larger than the body. Throughout the entire pregnancy, termination was presented as an option. I assured the doctors and nurses that even if my child was born with disabilities he was mine and a gift from God. There was no proof that anything was wrong with my baby, nor did the medical staff have answers for what was taking place. I saw a correlation with my and Elizabeth's and stories. At a time when Elizabeth and Zechariah should have been able to rejoice and share their excitement with each other but were not able to because he could not speak. My son's father and I should have been able to rejoice and be excited, but we were forced to consider that our pregnancy was full of complications. The chain of events made each appointment taxing for both of us., as I imagine the communication barrier was for Elizabeth and Zechariah's relationship. It must have been a major pain to not be able to have the planning conversations parents have when they are welcoming a new baby. I can only imagine that Elizabeth was still very grateful to be blessed with a child after feeling that she would never be able to have the experience.

My doctor's appointments were 4 times a week. I dreaded each and every one of them. I felt as if they wanted me to terminate my pregnancy. I got the impression that they felt there was no place for my child if he was not whole by society's standards. Thanks to the support of my mother and son's father, I was reminded that he was a gift from God and we served a just God. My mom told me that she did not believe in her heart and spirit that God would have brought me this far to leave me. At one of the appointments, I was mandated to go to the hospital where I would have some observations completed. Within an hour my miracle baby was born at 28 weeks and 6 days at 1lb, 15oz. For the next three months, the focus was on what my baby needed to live: blood platelets, a ventilator, a CPAP machine to help him breathe, feeding tubes, and head IVs. All I could do was pray that God would see us both through; He was in control. Psalm 46:10, "Be still and know that I am God," was constantly on my mind.

Like God's promise to Elizabeth with her son John, my son was here and perfectly mine. Besides prayer, I did the only other thing I could for my precious miracle: feed him. I pumped breast milk every 3 to 4 hours, no matter what. Between that and trips back and forth to the hospital, my days seemed to never end. With the Lord's guidance, I was able to make important decisions about his care. I did not have a medical degree. I knew nothing about nursing. But God showed up and showed out every single day for those 3 months. I knew God had me, and I had our son. Our son was released home from the hospital after 3 months and is now 7 years old without any health defects, major breathing issues, or hearing issues.

God loved Elizabeth so much that regardless of the odds against her, He allowed her to experience the miracle of giving birth. God is a faithful and never-failing God. His timing is perfect. We are often failed by the promises of man, but our Father in heaven keeps every promise. When we believe in Him, they all come to pass. Trust that your Father has your best interest at heart. He is looking out for you. Even when it is hard, keep pushing, pressing, and believing. All things are possible through our Lord and Savior.

Pray this prayer with me
Before You formed me in the womb, You knew me; before I was born You set me apart. (Jeremiah 1:5) God, I am looking to You for miracles, signs, and wonders. I know, that I know, that I know, You are more than able to provide my hearts' desires

that align with Your will. You know my heart and You know my desires. So, please guide me in Your will and show me Your way. Please provide me with Your sweet peace, grace, and strength. In Jesus name, Amen.

DAY 9

Real Life Royalty Requires Superhero Faith
(Esther)
— Clarissa Pritchett —

"For if you remain completely silent at this time, relief and deliverance will arise for the Jews from another place, but you and your father's house will perish. Yet who knows whether you have come to the kingdom for such a time as this?"
– Esther 4:14

GIRL, I DON'T know about you, but I love superheroes. Especially "sheroes" - women who are admired or idealized for their courage, outstanding achievements, or their noble qualities. Esther is one of my sheroes of the Bible. In my opinion, faith is her superpower. She truly started at the bottom and came up. She followed the calling God had on her life and made a difference. She saved the day for her people despite her life circumstances. I don't envy Esther's path to royalty at all, as it definitely does not paint a picture of a true love story and becoming a queen the way may women imagine what becoming a queen looks like in real life. Esther didn't enter into the Empire of Persia excited to be a queen in love with the king. Esther was a Jewish orphan, living in Persia, during a time when Jews and women were not valued. She was raised by her older cousin, Mordecai, a servant in the palace of King Xerxes. I know how hard it is growing up in a single-parent home, I cannot imagine what it was like for Esther growing up with her uncle who was a Jew and a servant.

Mordecai did his best to care for Esther while serving the King who seemed to have a big ego. King Xerxes seemed like a man who did not like being told no by his queen. He cared more about what the men in his court thought than what his Queen felt. One night, to make a point in front of his court, King Xerxes kicked Queen Vashti out of the palace after she disrespected him during a celebration and, on the advice of his counselors, decided to choose a new Queen. I don't know if Esther knew what was going on at the palace but after King Xerxes kicked Queen Vashti out of the palace, there was a mandate that went out to all the empire for women to be taken to the king's harem so that he could choose a new queen. Esther was one of the women taken into King Xerxes's harem. The dictionary states that in former times the harem was "the separate part of a Muslim household reserved for wives, concubines, and female servants." While in King Xerxes' harem Esther had to change her real Hebrew name from Hadassah to Esther, and keep her identity as a Jew a secret. Esther 2:12 (NIV) says, "Before a young woman's turn came to go into King Xerxes, she had to complete twelve months of beauty treatments prescribed for the women, six months with oil of myrrh and six with perfumes and cosmetics." It sounds like King Xerxes was basically trying out different women until he found a favorite to be his next queen. Esther went from being an orphan to being part of a harem for a year, all while keeping her identity a secret like most superheroes do. Esther 2:12 says, she "gained favor in the sight of everyone who saw her." King Xerxes chose Ester to become his next queen.

Queen Esther had to go through some "thangs" to become Queen. And that was just the beginning. God had a mission for Esther. After becoming the Queen, Esther had to learn what was required of her in her new role. She had to wait for the King to call on her to be seen by him. She could not approach him on her own terms.

Queen Esther's story then becomes filled with suspense as a bad guy, Haman, enters the picture. Haman was King Xerxes's right-hand man. One day Haman got upset that Queen Esther's cousin, Mordecai, refused to bow down to him. Haman became so angry that he convinced King Xerxes to order ALL Jews to be destroyed. At that point, Mordecai told Queen Esther that she had to do something about the situation. Queen Esther requested that her people fast with her for three days.

All Queen Esther had gone through in life up to that point had prepared her to fulfill her purpose. She made a bold decision to risk her life and go to King Xerxes without being called to do so, even though the penalty was death. King Xerxes allowed Queen Esther to speak and she made her request known to him. She used her superpower of faith and God showed up for her. King Xerxes ended up having Haman executed after he heard that he was planning to murder Mordecai and have all the Jews killed. A classic good vs. evil where the bad guy's plan fails. Esther did what she had to do at the right time. God used her life circumstances to save her people. God created her for a crown but her road to royalty was paved with sacrifice, risk, selflessness, bravery, and ultimate faith in God.

There were times in my life where I really questioned the circumstances into which I was born. My father committed suicide when I was three days old in front of my mom. My mom, who was from a Catholic family, was basically disowned because she had me out of wedlock. Growing up we were poor, plain and simple. People would drop off food on our doorstep. Girls made fun of me for the clothes I wore. I got pushed around a lot as a short girl. There was a period of time when I started to push back as well. I felt like I had to bully others in order to survive and avoid being bullied. I felt like I didn't have much of a choice in a lot of situations growing up. I wanted to do a lot of things that my mom could not afford so I watched other girls become cheerleaders, rock it on the dance team, and more. Wherever I lived, I hid. From small apartments to trailers, to an RV. I was in fear of being embarrassed in front of everyone, so I hid.

I was frequently underestimated because of my family's socio-economic status. By the time I got to high school, I was working really hard. I worked two jobs to pay for basic necessities, and save money for college. After school, I worked at the grocery store, and on the weekends, I worked cleaning houses but I kept it a secret. I became a social butterfly hiding everything I was going through. I was chosen as senior class president and even prom queen, but I struggled to keep a smile on my face. I ended up joining the military after graduation. and was selected for a full-ride college scholarship. I continued to work multiple jobs in college to make ends meet.

Today I am a Major with close to 19 years of service. The struggles and challenges didn't stop with coming up through the ranks. New and unfamiliar challenges came my way. I have had to speak out and choose many hard rights over easier wrongs. I've earned several titles, positions, and awards but all of that did not come without sacrifices. I may have not come from a distinguished family or the best circumstances but now I see God's hand in it all. God was preparing and strengthening my faith. Some of my girls call me superwoman and say they don't know how I did it. I love to give God all the credit for everything. Looking back, God showed me He had a plan for me all along and that real-life royalty isn't always sitting pretty in a castle with a shining crown without life struggles. I'll never forget where I come from and what God has brought me through. I only pray that I can inspire and encourage others to do the same showing how God loved me enough to help me succeed during difficult times. I remember hearing the quote, "God does not call the qualified, He qualifies the called." I believe we are all queens called for a purpose in life.

What about you? Have you ever felt like your circumstances kept you from accomplishing something extraordinary in life? Do you look at other women as queens and superwomen instead of looking at the queen and superhero within you? Do you know God has created you for a crown despite your past and where you come from? I want to remind you that it is not about where we are from;

it's about where God is taking you. The struggle may be real, but so is God. He loves you during every struggle and will not leave your side. With super faith, you may have already been a shero in someone else's life facing that "for such a time as this" moment or that moment may still be coming for you. Keep the faith, Queen, and continue doing the right thing no matter what. You have a sister in Christ right here cheering for you!

Pray this Prayer with Me
God, strengthen my faith and give me confidence in you daily. Help me trust that You take those in the world that others pass up and use them for an incredible purpose. Give my heart strength to endure the struggles and give You glory for the victories You will help me win. Equip me to be brave and bold and live in faith over fear. Help me fast for spiritual stamina and stand tall in the presence of my enemies. Help me do what is right no matter the cost. Thank you for creating me for a crown as I know it will shine for bright for You

DAY 10

Prepared Just for You!
(Eve)
— Allison Denise Arnett —

"Then the Lord God made the rib He had taken from the man into a woman and brought her to the man."
– Genesis 2:22 HSCB

MOTHER OF CIVILIZATION. The first woman. The first wife. The first mother. Wife of Adam. The woman deceived by Satan who ate the apple. The reason we have pain during childbearing and must answer to our husbands. These are some of the things you might think of when you hear the name Eve. Eve was many things. What I remember most about Eve is that she was a prepared helpmate for a prepared partner and a prepared place. It may appear that she was an afterthought. Like God was feeling His way through creation however I believe God was intentional about her placement in the story.

It's an amazing feeling when people make a big deal over us. How much more amazing when God makes a big deal over us. I can't say I have often experienced this with people, but I can definitely say I have experienced it with God. I remember for my fortieth birthday. Some of the women in my family had secretly conspired together to surprise me for my special day. They prepared a day comprised of a visit to the spa, a full body massage, a pedicure, my favorite music, lunch, and birthday cake. They gathered everyone who was available to join the festivities. I shed tears of joy at the thought that they had gone through all of this for me! The effort must have taken. The countless texts and calls. The keeping of the secret until its appropriate time. The careful consideration of what would bring me joy and so much more.

We often talk about Adam's response to seeing his new woman for the first time, but can you imagine how Eve may have felt upon opening her eyes for the first time? Imagine waking to the perfect place, the perfect partner, at the perfect time. Imagine looking around and seeing "every tree pleasing in appearance and good for food," all the wild animals and birds of the sky. The Bible says that when God was finished forming Eve, He brought her to Adam. She didn't have to go looking for anything. She didn't have to try to figure out what was going on. No; God placed her in the protection of a man that was filled with His Spirit, that could teach her all that God had taught him, and would bless her with a name. I can almost hear the Spirit within her singing, "God, you did all of this for me?!?!"

Queen, you are both fearfully and wonderfully made in the image of the Creator of Heaven and Earth. Do you know how many individual and unique things since the beginning of time had to be set in motion just for you to come into existence? Just for your father and mother to cross paths to be the gateway for you. And while your parents may have been great, it was God who formed you in your mother's womb (Jeremiah 1:5). Queen, He took the time and effort to count the hairs on your head (Luke 12:7). When I consider this for myself, all I can say is, "God, you did all of this for me?!?!" And I hear Him replying. "Yes ma'am. You mean that much to me. So much so that I prepared all of this for you!" Can you see all that God has prepared for you? Look past the pain, disappointment, shame, hurt, and see the purpose and preparation in your life. God didn't go through all He did to bring you here for nothing. All things work together for good. "As it is written, Eye hath not seen, nor ear heard, neither have entered into the heart of man, the things which God hath prepared for them that love him." (1 Corinthians 2:9 KJV) Will you let Him show you what He has prepared for you? And when

He does, will you receive it?

Pray this prayer with me:
Father God, forgive me for not understanding all that You have prepared for me. Lord, I am so joyfully grateful to come into an understanding that I am a prepared woman for prepared blessings. And now God, I open my eyes to see, my ears to hear, and my heart to understand all that You have prepared for me. I know that I am worthy to receive it all. The fact that You made me qualifies me. Hallelujah! Thank You Jesus for all You have done for me. I receive it all now. In Jesus' name. Amen. And it is so!

I've Been Cheating on God
(Gomer)
— Jessica Jená Green —

"Then the Lord said to me, "Go again; show love to a woman who is loved by another man and is an adulteress, just as the Lord loves the Israelites though they turn to other gods and love raisin cakes."
– Hosea 3:1

THE BOOK OF Hosea illustrates God's faithful love to a group of unfaithful people. The book of Hosea is the story of God and Israel. It is also our love story and could be applied today. As God begins to speak through Hosea, He instructs him to marry a prostitute named Gomer. The fact that God told Hosea to marry a prostitute should be a sweet reminder, that God can use anyone, with any past, in any capacity to carry out his purpose! The marriage of Hosea and Gomer is used as a symbol of God's love for his adulterous people. He wanted to illustrate how Israel had acted like a prostitute by turning against the Lord and worshipping other gods.

As women, we often run to other things and people to fill the voids that life's circumstances tend to inflict on us. Somewhat like the people of Israel described in Hosea, we run after things that were never meant to be caught. We search for things that God doesn't want us to find. We give away pieces of ourselves to people and things that God never intended for us. We shop to avoid dealing with some of our responsibilities. We surround ourselves with others to avoid spending the necessary one on one time that is necessary and crucial with ourselves and with God. We spend countless hours on social media to avoid reality causing unwarranted feelings of comparison, self-doubt, and sometimes jealousy. Sis, God wants you to return to your first true love today. He wants you to return to Him.

"Then the Lord said to me, "Go again; show love to a woman who is loved by another man and is an adulteress, just as the Lord loves the Israelites though they turn to other gods and love raisin cakes." Hosea 3:1 God wants you to remember that no matter how far you stray, no matter how many times you run to other things He is waiting for you to return to Him. Not only is He waiting for you, but His arms are also wide open and He still loves you. God is waiting for you to accept His unfailing love and compassion. He wants you to live in the peace and safety that can be found in Him. He wants you to know Him as your Lord. One thing I've learned over the years is that no one or nothing can satisfy me the way that God can. His love is untouchable! Tap into it today.

Pray this prayer with me:

God, today I choose to return to You. I return my heart to You God. I return my mind, my desires, my needs, and wants to You. I repent for making other things and people my idols and allowing them to take over the spot in my heart that belongs to You. God, as I return fully to you, I pray that I prosper in every way and I continue to enjoy good health as my soul prospers. (3 John 1:2) God help me to walk in the fullness of You. Help me to depend more on Your character and unfailing love than I do the things of this world. Thank you, God, for Your faithfulness even during my moments of unfaithfulness. In Jesus name, I pray, Amen.

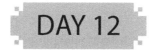
Choosing Faith Over Fear!
(Hagar)
— Tiffany LaGrone —

For my thoughts are not your thoughts, neither are your ways my ways, saith the LORD. For as the heavens are higher than the earth, so are my ways higher than your ways and thoughts than your thoughts.
– Isaiah 55:8-9

DOING ALL YOU can do to help others can be a strain. When reading about Hagar and all she went through, working as a slave, being used, and abused I find myself wondering if all of this was for a purpose. Reliving the memories of a tragedy that became a triumph.

Working long hours, putting in the extra work even when I felt unappreciated made it hard to focus on the good things. In those dark times, I found myself wondering if God was really interested in what I was going through. Having to be used in ways that are unsettling, I tried to imagine the positive part about it all. Psalms 55:22 states "Cast thy burden upon the LORD, and he shall sustain thee: he shall never suffer the righteous to be moved." In all of that, God heard my cry and took me out of a situation just for a moment. He knows the suffering of his people. Romans 8:18 states. "For I reckon that the suffering of this present time are not worthy to be compared with the glory which shall be revealed in us."

Everything happens for a reason. Sending Hagar away allowed

God to speak to her and let her know the plan he had for her and her son. His promise is His promise. Isaiah 55:11 states "So shall my word be that goeth forth out of my mouth; it shall not return unto me void, but it shall accomplish that which I please, and it shall prosper in the thing whereto I sent it." Sometimes God has to put us in an uncomfortable spot in order to get our attention.

Thinking back, I had to remember there were times I felt I was in a dry place. I would pray for the healing of my daughter, she was born with a slight disability. When I didn't see a change, I thought that maybe my prayers weren't being answered because of all my past. I cried out and God heard me. I was told that my daughter was going to be a powerful woman of God and her ability (disability) was the key to ministering to others. When we find ourselves in a dry place just know that God is there. 1 Kings 8:57 states "The LORD our God be with us, as he was with our fathers: let him not leave us, or forsake us:" Now after several years of therapy my daughter is blessed. She graduated from high school. God's plan will come to pass.

Jeremiah 29:11 states "For I know the thoughts that I think toward you, saith the LORD, thoughts of peace, and not of evil, to give you an expected end."

Pray this prayer with me:
Father God I thank You for Your word. It comforts us and allows us to remember Your promises for our lives. Continue to speak to us in our dry place. We ask all of this in Your Holy Name. Amen.

DAY 13

Mamma Bear Faith
(Hannah)
— Clarissa Pritchett —

"He grants the barren woman a home, like a joyful mother of children."
– Psalm 113:9

HAVE YOU EVER poured your heart out to God for something you wanted? I surely have. I remember soaking my pillows at night wondering if God was hearing my prayers, wondering if I was worthy of what I was asking for. In the book of Samuel, we find the story of Hannah who desperately wanted a child but her womb was barren. She was married to Elkanah who also had another wife named Peninnah who had children. Peninnah was petty and threw it in Hannah's face that she had children. The story kind of sounds like modern-day "other baby momma" drama problems.

Nevertheless, Hannah did not let Peninnah's pettiness stop her from praying and having faith in God. Hannah continued asking God for a child and believing that He would bless her with a son. Hannah prayed so hard one time that Eli, a priest, heard her and thought she was drunk. She explained to Eli that she was crying out to God for a child. In 1 Samuel 1:11, Hannah prayed, "Lord Almighty, if you will only look on your servant's misery and remember me, and not forget your servant but give her a son, then I will give him to the Lord for all the days of his life…" After that, Hannah waited on God. At the perfect time, God Blessed Hannah with a son named Samuel who had an extraordinary purpose for his time. Hannah was also blessed with five more children. Amen! Hannah was blessed with more than what she asked for with her "momma bear" faith.

I always wanted a family of my own. Ten-year plans were written in my goal book to get a degree, get a good job, work hard, get married, and start a family. In 2004, I was on my third year of serving in the Army National Guard and working to complete my bachelor's degree. I started having severe and intolerable back pain. I never really went to see a doctor growing up, and being in the military, I had a motto of "suck it up and drive on." However, I couldn't take the pain and "drive on" anymore.

I decided to schedule a doctor's appointment at the student health center on campus in between classes. It was finals week. I was hoping for some painkillers and sleep during winter break. The physician assistant (PA) I saw suspected I may have a cyst on my ovary. As an extra precaution, the PA sent me to a women's specialty clinic to get an ultrasound. It turned out I had two tumors on one of my ovaries. My ovary was the size of a grapefruit and putting pressure on my back causing the pain. I ended up in emergency surgery to remove the tumors and spent winter break in bed. I was devastated. I could not believe what I was going through. It all happened so fast.

The healing process was extremely painful physically, mentally, and emotionally. I distinctly remember the doctor telling me that my chances of having children would be slim to none. I still couldn't believe it. I had things all planned out in my goal book and it didn't seem like God cared about my sacrifices, my prayers as a child, or my grown college woman plans at all. Although, having children wasn't something I wanted at that time, I was "shook" about the future. Feelings of fear and inadequacy crept up on me and I was worried about what my future would look like. I felt like I did something wrong in life to deserve the news of possibly never having children. I poured my heart out to God and asked Him for peace. God turned me back to my goal book where I had the word B.E.A.R written down with "Belief. Energy. Action. Results."

I ended up changing my degree from nursing to health and nutrition, and I continued to focus on school and my career. I changed my prayer life, my faith life, and my diet. As years passed, I would see girls I went to school with getting married and having children. I would have other women say things to me like "you aren't married yet?" or "girl, you better have kids soon before you get too old." I'm sure those women were not trying to be petty like Peninnah in Hannah's story, but their comments hit hard.

Six years later in God's time, He blessed me with a hubby who accepted that I may not have children. After our first year of marriage, I got pregnant with our first son. Let me tell you, I took eleven home pregnancy tests before I scheduled an appointment to take a test at the doctor's office. Labor was rough, to say the least, but meeting our baby "boo" bear for the first time I felt like Hannah when she said "For this boy I prayed, and the LORD has given me my petition which I asked of Him," in 1 Samuel 1:27. Today I'm a "momma bear" of three boys. God gave me more than what I asked for. I'm thankful God heard my prayers and I stayed focused on my momma bear faith. I've been able to minister to other women that have had the same female health issues with ovarian tumors and help them with proper diet, preparation, and prayer to try and have children.

Sometimes no news or bad news comes and can weaken our faith. Other times we may have people say things that punch us in the gut when we are waiting on God. We may feel God is not hearing our prayers. Maybe it is not a child at all that we are praying for. Birthing a business, book, or big goal might be what we desire. Circumstances may make it seem impossible as we see others having what we want when we have been praying and waiting a long time. But we can continue to have "momma bear" faith that God is always listening. We can trust God is always on time ready to bless us with more than what we ask for when we put Him first.

Pray this prayer with me

Father God, thank You so much for loving me and hearing my prayers. Please let the desires of my heart come from You to fulfill my purpose. Give me momma bear faith to trust in You, Your perfect will, and timing. In Jesus' Name, Amen.

DAY 14

More Than A Woman, You Are A Warrior!
(Jael)
— Brejette Terry-Emery —

"Be on your guard; stand firm in the faith; be courageous; be strong."
– 1 Corinthians 16:13

THE VICTORIOUS STORY of Jael is found in the Book of Judges. Jael was the wife of Heber who had separated from the Kenites and pitched a tent in Zaanaim. At this time Israel was at war with the Canaanites. Deborah, wife of Lapidoth, sends Barak to fight the Canaanites. Jael's fate is prophesied by Deborah who foretold that Sisera would not fall in battle to Barak but to a woman.

During the war Sisera, the Canaanite general breaks free from the battle with general Barak and finds himself in the tent of Jael. Sisera thought he would be safe because there was a peace treaty between his king and the Kenites. Jael welcomed Sisera in and began to tend to him. She provided him with milk and a warm place to rest.

Sisera demands Jael to take guard and to cover for him in the event that someone was looking for him. When he falls asleep, Jael takes Sisera's life by driving a tent rod into his head and into the floor of the tent.

Others will often underestimate your capabilities as a woman, but all things are possible through God who strengthens you. As women, we grow up watching Disney movies and reading fairy tales. We are programmed to believe that the calling of a woman is to be a wife and a mother. The persona of perfection and superwoman is instilled in us early. The perception is that if you are a real woman you should be able to juggle it all. These ideas introduce us to unrealistic expectations. Jael was a woman that came from what was thought to be a peaceful people. She seemed to have a nurturing spirit. The expectation was that she would follow the expected norm. As for me, I found myself a stepmother at the age of 17 years old. I pushed through the expectations of my parents and family to complete high school and then college. Another baby was conceived by my partner at the time, but it was not with me. The pressure was on to walk away and to fall apart but I decided that I would stick it out.

Social norms expect women to be married before having children. At the age of 22, I became a wife with 3 stepsons whom I love dearly. I envision Jael following her daily duties and what was expected of her from her family. I envision others looking to her as the lady that was able to hold it all together. Others looked to me as a weak, young, naive girl. What did they know? They had never walked a mile in my shoes. I was a young woman that sought to be loved in my entirety. I was willing to understand the deeper issues in the situations that would later leave me lost and in deep pain. At the age of 24, I just knew this was my fairy tale turn; I found out that I was pregnant with my first child. I would now be seen as a woman, right? His woman, his wife, his forever? I would bare his child and now become his priority, as he and the stepsons had been mine. I became a full time working mother and wife. I was able to provide for my family. Was this my purpose? Was this the calling on my life? I was overweight, highly stressed, working to live, and living to work. At the age of 27, I found myself bawling in my closet with my then 3-year-old sitting at my side. He looked up to me and said, "Mom what are we going to do now?" The last 10 years flashed through my mind and the life that I knew was over. What was next? I think about Jael in her tent with Sisera. I see Jael in the moment tending to this man who was exhausted and sleeping in her tent. I see her wanting to provide him with empathy and sympathy as that was the expectation of her from society. I see her being overwhelmed with the stench of death, hatred, pain, and bondage that came from Sisera's pores and lingered in the air.

As I sat in that closet and contemplated ending it all, this scripture came to my remembrance: "Fear not, for I am with you; be not dismayed, for I am your God; I will strengthen you, I will help you, I will uphold you with my righteous right hand." Isaiah 41:10 I heard God's voice asking, "What will he do without you? Who will love him like you? Who will teach him the importance of life, and all the lessons you have learned from the death, pain, hatred, and bondage in your soul?" God said, "Get up! "Come to me, all who labor and are heavy laden, and I will give you rest." Matthew 11:28 I had carried so much in those eleven years that God saw fit that I be released. Jael must have found in her heart that this was her chance to free a people that had suffered great slavery and oppression. If not her, who? When? As Jael took Sisera's life, I envision that being a time in her life where she was released and arose all at the same time. She rose up and became a warrior. Through my pain and strife, I was able to gain rest and rise. I became the warrior of my life and all that I had endured. Something had to end or die for me to be released and so I could rise. Life as I had known it had to die so that I could live. That was the start of my inspiration and empowerment journey. I found myself posting and sharing videos as I talked to myself through my pain. I told myself what I needed to hear to push through. "I can do all things through him who strengthens me." Philippians 4:13

God loved Jael so much that he allowed her to be more than a woman but to be seen as a warrior. The many painful experiences and life lessons I have experienced have not kept me from moving forward. I am using them to uplift others. God sees us as more than a social norm or the expectations of society on our lives. We are more than a woman, we are worriers. God sees your struggle and knows your pain. He knows your heart. I want you to know that you are not alone. God is right there with you. Call on him! He is waiting for you.

Pray this prayer with me:

I will trust in the Lord with all my heart, and not lean on my own understanding. In all my ways I will acknowledge him, and He will make straight my path. (Proverbs 3: 5-6) Thank you, Father God, for reminding me that I am not alone. Thank you for Your protection, grace, and mercy. For I am not worthy but You know my purpose and the calling You have on my life. Show me the way in which I should go. I will walk by faith and not by sight knowing that You will not allow me to fall but to learn. Thank you, Father God. Amen.

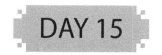

DAY 15

Sis You Can Overcome
(Job's Wife)
— Min. Vickey Neal —

While he was yet speaking, there came also another, and said, Thy sons and thy daughters were eating and drinking wine in their eldest brother's house: And, behold, there came a great wind from the wilderness, and smote the four corners of the house, and it fell upon the young men, and they are dead; and I only am escaped alone to tell thee. Then Job arose, and rent his mantle, and shaved his head, and fell down upon the ground, and worshipped,
– Job 1:18-20

THE BIBLE REMINDS us of the words that Jesus spoke in John 16:33(KJV). That in me you might have peace. In the world you shall have tribulation: but be of good cheer; I have overcome the world.

God had blessed Job and his wife with 10 children, servants, farm, and cattle. Through a test that was placed upon her husband's life allowed by God, Job and his wife lost everything they cared about, all in one day. In spite of losing everything they had, Job kept his faith in God even while his body was struck with a disease. Job was so hurt that he cursed the day he was born. Job was very innocent and had not deserved the curse upon him. There was a time that Job would say "God is a just God", then he doubted God's goodness. His wife stood strong by his side for years. She adored him but now she couldn't watch Job suffer much longer. She told Job to just curse God and die. Then she fell to her knees and cried. Job's wife spoke like a foolish woman.

Sis, we all have lost someone or something and endured grief or depression. There is a way out of the emotional rollercoaster. We can take the high road and release it to God or vent to a friend. It's ok, Sis, to talk to a trusted friend and release whatever is going on in our life that we aren't in agreement with. The wrong step is taking the low road, blaming God for what is wrong.

I was very close to my mother as a teenager into adulthood. One day God called my mother home. I had plans for her to be a part of my son's life. I was expecting my first child at the time of her death. Yes, it hurt me to know that she was never able to be a grandmother to my son. Yes, it hurt me that she was walking around and spending time with me one day, and the next day she's gone. I knew that I had to give that hurt to God and let Him comfort me. (Matthew 11:28) "Come to me, all who labor and are heavy laden, and I will give you rest". This is the very scripture that helped me through that season. Sis, having that relationship with God helped me understand that He does things for a reason and that He is also a comforter in the time of need.

Sister, our life can seem to carry lots of twists and turns, ups and downs. Sometimes In the middle of it all just take a deep breath and say, "I am still breathing". Then count it all joy and use every mistake or wrong decision as a footstool to just climb up. You overcome one obstacle, then another; you got this, Sis. (Ecclesiastes 9:11) The race is not given to the swift nor the strong but those who endure to the end. At this point, you begin to understand that allowing the enemy to push you into blaming God and cursing Him for the challenges you face, is not an option. God will give you strength to overcome all those obstacles and you will see that you still have life. God created us to be so unique and strong. He created us in his image (Genesis 1:27). Establish a prayer life with him to gain even more trust in him.

Pray this prayer with me:
Dear God, I know that You will not withhold any good thing from

me if I walk uprightly. So, today I give You my time. I give You my life to better serve You. I understand that You are the Author and the Finisher of my faith. I know that as I walk this journey that I am not walking it alone. So, therefore, I will acknowledge You in all my ways and allow You to direct my path. I will accept what You allow in my life. Amen.

DAY 16

Mysteries of Destiny
(Jochebed, Moses Mom)
— Tiffany LaGrone —

These things I have spoken unto you, that in me ye might have peace.
In the world ye shall have tribulation: but be of good cheer;
I have overcome the world.
– John 16:33

A MOTHER'S JOB is always important and yet not done. We cook and clean. Most of us work to provide for our family. A mother's work is never complete or so we think.

Reading the bible and learning about the different women that stood strong and had faith, made me think about Jochebed, mother of Aaron, Miriam, and Moses. When Pharaoh used the Hebrews as slaves and forced them to work in the heat. Times were very hard. Pharaoh wanted to make sure that Hebrew baby boys were killed. Now Jochebed knowing this couldn't bear to see her baby Moses killed so she hid him for three months. When she couldn't hide him anymore, she put him in a basket and pushed him to the river banks.

Isaiah 54:17 states "No weapon that is formed against thee shall prosper; and every tongue that shall rise against thee in judgment thou shalt condemn. This is the heritage of the servants of the Lord, and their righteousness is of me, saith the Lord."
Sounds familiar! How many of us can say that life sometimes wants to destroy our children? As a mother knowing the danger,

you have to let your children go and watch God protect them. Just like God watched over Moses in the river. God blessed Jochebed to even take care of her own child. Wow! Isn't that amazing how God will use your enemies to be a blessing to you? The plans God has for us are great. We might not understand how and why we have to travel the route given to us but we know it's worth the trip.

Proverbs 3: 3-6 "Let not steadfast love and faithfulness forsake you; bind them around your neck; write them on the tablet of your heart. So you will find favor and good success in the sight of God and man. Trust in the Lord with all your heart, and do not lean on your own understanding. "In all your ways acknowledge Him, and He will make straight your path.

Pray this prayer with me:
Father God, I thank You for all the mothers that sacrifice a lot for their family. I ask that You continue to guide them every day of their lives. In Jesus name. Amen.

DAY 17

Rejected by your Spouse and All in the House
(Leah)
— Patti Denise Henry —

"Leah was tender eyed; but Rachel was beautiful and well favored."
— Genesis 29:17

LEAH ENTERS OUR story and before we were even allowed to form our own opinion of her, she was introduced as weak-eyed, unattractive, undesirable, and pale in comparison to her younger sister. Nothing was mentioned of her character, her faith, her desire to worship God, and serve her father. It is difficult to single her out in this story as she was positioned between two very strong characters. She enters the text juxtaposed to her youngest sister which was an obvious losing battle from the start.

Tender-eyed Leah lived in a home where she was reminded every day that she was a stumbling block. She was scorned, rejected, ridiculed, and overlooked. I imagine that suitor after suitor would come to seek marriage to her younger sister, Rachel, and would be denied because it was customary for the older sister to be given in marriage first. This led to sibling rivalry and animosity in the house. Leah's own father viewed her as a burden as he was saddled with the responsibility of caring for both daughters until they were married.

One of the leading characters in this story was a man named Jacob. He had fled his troubled past and was searching for his Uncle Laban, the brother of his mother Rebekah. On his journey, he came upon a few shepherds as they herded their flock around a well. He inquired of them and learned that the well belonged to his uncle. It was at that well where he laid his eyes upon Rachel for the first time and immediately fell in love with her. After an exchange of introductions, Rachel ran on ahead to tell her father about her encounter at the well.

A month had gone by when Laban offered to pay Jacob for his services. Jacob, in love with Rachel, offered to work for seven years in exchange for her hand in marriage. A sinister plot ensued and instead of Rachel, (Laban) Leah's father tricked Jacob by switching daughters on the wedding night. The next morning when the plot was revealed, Jacob confronted Laban about the unfairness of the act. Jacob made his discontent with Leah very clear. He truly loved her sister Rachel and did not appreciate Laban's deception. To make matters worse, Laban bargained for another seven years of labor before he would allow Jacob to marry Rachel.

Can you imagine how difficult it must have been to exchange a celebration for despair and rejection? Leah found herself trying many ways to earn the love of her husband and the respect of her family.

When the Lord saw that Leah was hated in her own house by her own husband and younger sister, He had a heart for her and opened her womb. She gave thanks to God for blessing her because of her affliction. Her sister Rachel was barren. Leah assumed that her husband would love her now that she had given him a son but that was not so. God's love and favor were on Leah and she gave birth to four sons for her husband. Her insatiable appetite for love and acceptance from Jacob prevented her from feeling and receiving God's love. It was not until the birth of her fourth son, Judah, that she finally stopped seeking love from Jacob and began to praise God.

Because of the affliction and abuses I had suffered during my formative years, I found myself empty and trying to prove how worthy I was to receive love. I was inoculated with so much self-criticism that it was difficult for me to even find anything praiseworthy within my own self. I became a performer. I could not even Identify what my needs were. I kept requiring from others the type of love, healing, and fulfillment that only God could give me. My sister, if you are reading this, I want you to know what I found out after all those years of emptiness. God was there all the time. Your experiences may be comparable to Leah's or even to mine or they may be worse. I'm here to let you know that God has been with you and will always be with you. His love is not forceful. He is patiently waiting for you to understand that He sees you as fearfully and wonderfully made. He had a heart for Leah. and He has a heart for me and you.

It was never recorded that Leah received validation from her husband or her family but she became content with her praise to God. She would not realize that the four sons she gave birth to would end up being powerful tribes of Israel. Out of her son, Levi came the Levitical priesthood, and Jesus Christ was descended from the line of her son Judah. Jesus Christ is the Lion of the tribe of Judah. We later find in Genesis 49: 29-41, that at the end of Jacob's life he requested to be buried with his grandfather and grandmother (Abraham & Sarah), with his parents (Isaac and Rebekah), and with his wife Leah, whom he had already buried there.

Affirmation: I am loved and accepted by the Creator of this universe.

Pray this prayer with me:
Dear God, you are the Father and Creator of all. There is nothing that you made that you did not call good. I realize that I have been looking for you for a long time. I have searched for you

in the eyes and the hearts of people that I have met. I have struggled with trying to be validated and never felt that I belonged. Father, I want to thank you for opening my eyes to the pure, perfect and unfailing love that you have for me. I now lift up a praise to you God. I lift up a voice of gratitude expressing to you that I am satisfied with you. Thank you, God, for being the love of my life. Amen.

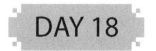
Sis, Don't Miss Your Blessing
By Looking Back
(Lot's Wife)
— Brittaney Pleasant —

"But Lot's wife looked back as she was following behind him, and
she turned into a pillar of salt."
– Genesis 19:26 NLT

HER NAME IS not mentioned in the Bible, but there is so much we
can learn from Lot's wife and the story of Sodom and Gomorrah.
Sodom was a wicked place filled with so much sin that the outcry
from the city prompted God to come see what was going on for
Himself. Lot's uncle, Abraham, pleaded with God to spare the city
for the sake of ten righteous people who may be found in the city.
Though ten righteous people were not found, God was gracious and
merciful enough to protect Lot and his family from the destruction
of the city because of Lot's willingness to protect the angels that
were sent to destroy it. They were instructed to run and escape to a
nearby city. The only catch was they were not to look back or stop in
the valley. As the story goes, Lot's wife did indeed look back and she
turned into a pillar of salt.

How absolutely sad is that? Lot's wife missed the promise and
protection of God because she disobeyed and looked back on the
city that was being destroyed. Not only did she look back, but the
scripture implies that she was behind her husband. I don't know
about you but if the Lord was destroying my hometown and told
me to take my family, run, and don't look back, I probably would

have been the first one headed for the hills and my family may have had to catch up with me! I'm just saying. Unfortunately, that was not the case for Lot's wife.

How many times have you suffered a similar fate? I hate to admit that it has happened to me more times than I care to remember. Of course, I didn't turn into a pillar of salt, but there were times God was calling me out of different situations, and I hesitated. I recall a particular relationship that was extremely toxic and abusive. I clearly heard God telling me to let the relationship go. Yet I procrastinated because I was convinced I could "love the hell out of him." In this case, it came at the cost of my own destruction. I left, and I even went back because as bad as it was some days, I didn't want to leave what was familiar to me. Perhaps this is also why Lot's wife looked back. All I did was delay what God had for me. I actually caused myself even more pain.

Sis, is this you? If it is, please do yourself a favor and let go. If God is calling you out of something, know that it doesn't matter if you don't know what the other side looks like. When you know the heart of God, you know that He only desires the best for us. Jeremiah 29:11 tells us, "For I know the plans I have for you," says the Lord. "They are plans for good and not for disaster, to give you a future and a hope." Even when you don't know what to expect, rest in the fact that God knows sis. He desires to give us His best, but how can He do that when we keep looking back at the very thing He wants us to let go of?

Pray this prayer with me:

Dear Heavenly Father, I pray you would show me your heart for me. I pray that you would help me to see that you only desire what is best for me and you have plans to give me a future full of hope and good things. Help me to trust you enough to look forward into the beautiful future you have for me without looking back at what I have become used to. Help me to let go of my past so that you may do a new thing in my life. In Jesus name, I pray, amen.

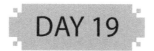

Sis, even though you are busy, always have time for God!
(Lydia)
— Clarice May Cregger —

"Her faith was born through hearing the Word of God"
– (Psalm 119:18,130)
"Not Slothful in business, Fervent in Spirit, Serving the Lord"
– (Romans 12:11)

THIS IS A story about a woman in the bible named Lydia of Thyatira. She was a well-known business owner dealing in textiles colored with the purple dye for which her region was famous for. Her wealth allowed her to live independently in her own home. She became a worshipper of God when Paul and Silas came to her city. God opened her heart to hear what they were saying. Then she was baptized along with her entire household. Even with all her business success, she opened her home to all the apostles that traveled through her city. Her home allowed the believers to have daily fellowship. God loved her so much that he blessed her because of her eagerness to build that relationship with Him, and her obedience to know him and her passion to be a blessing to others.

All of us at one point in our lives have had or we currently have dreams. For me, that dream was to own my own business. As a child, I wondered if I could do it. Now, as a business owner, I can relate to Lydia's story. I am sure you can too. I remember growing up wondering what it really means to own your own business. At that time, I did not really have a full understanding of God or how He could help me. All I knew was that I wanted to know Him, I wanted a relationship with him. Lydia's story is so inspiring because even though she fulfilled her dreams of being a business owner, and was able to live in her own home, she knew in her heart that something was still missing, and that was a deeper relationship with God. Oftentimes, we get so caught up with achieving our dreams and goals in life that we forget God is the center of it all. God is so good that he made a way for her to get to know Him. He even used her to bless others to show everyone the love God has for all of us.

God loves us so much that he wants to have a relationship with you. He wants to have a relationship with you. He wants to get to know you. God knows what is in your heart. He knows your dreams and goals, and He wants to fulfill those dreams for you. God knows His plans for you. Jeremiah 29:11 tells us that God's plan is to prosper us, not to harm us and he wants to give us hope and a plan for our future. If we hold on to His promise life gets a lot clearer. We have the help we need to stay on course and not be so easily distracted. This is a lesson I wish I had learned earlier as I started my own business. I was very stubborn, and I leaned on my own understanding instead of consulting the Lord and asking for His guidance. I got hurt a lot, felt defeated, betrayed, and lost my sense of hope. It took all this pain for me to realize that I am not in control, that He is my provider, and that I must seek Him first in everything. I do, in both my personal and business life. So, I challenge you to let go and let God. Trust the process and watch him unfold the calling and purpose on your life, just as he did for Lydia.

Pray this prayer with me:
God, I come to You in full surrender and humbleness, trusting You with all my heart, instead of leaning on my own understanding. I pray that I place my trust and acknowledge You in all my ways, that guide me to, and in, the path You have set before me. Amen (Proverbs 3:5-6)

DAY 20

There's Purpose in The Process
(Manoah's Wife)
— Shneice L. Hurd —

"Now let thy words come to pass. How shall we order the child,
and how shall we do unto him?"

— Judges 13:12

IN THIS STORY, Manoah's barren wife was visited by an angel. The angel told her she would bear a child, and also explained what she needed to abstain from while carrying her child. Manoah's wife received what the angel was telling her without hesitation. She was told the child she carried was going to deliver Israel from the Philistines. She went to tell her husband everything the angel said, and they asked for the angel to appear again. When the angel appeared again, they said the following: "Now let thy words come to pass. How shall we order the child, and how shall we do unto him?" Judges 13:12 They wanted to be sure to follow God's instructions. They recognized what had been entrusted to them by God.

The instructions Manoah's wife was given to follow reminds me of the beginning of my journey with Christ. As important as it is to ask God for direction in our walk with Him, I've learned it's equally important to learn to trust the process. The word process means a series of actions or steps taken in order to achieve a particular end. On this journey, I've gone through a range of emotions, and moments of extreme uncertainty. Deciding to live for Christ was so different from the path I was on, and I was obviously treading on unfamiliar territory. Some of the people I was used to being around suddenly were not as close anymore. Initially, I struggled to accept it. However, as time passed, I learned just as Manoah's wife had, to abstain from certain things in order for the baby she would carry to grow into his purpose. That was exactly what God was doing in me.

When we look at ourselves at the beginning of our journey, we're unclear of what our purpose is until we begin to go through the process. Although it can be scary and intimidating, understand God is with you! I had chapters in my life I call the 'Why me?' phase. Can you relate? I thought I was always getting the short end of the stick. I felt like I just could not catch a break. Over time I began to realize through each trial I faced God did not allow it to overtake me. He did not leave me to face the trials alone. He was there to wipe every tear and guide me safely through. Looking back over my journey I look at everything I've gone through as a new achievement to add to my spiritual resume. I was amazed at the strength God had placed inside me and humbled by every victory I experienced. I must admit at times it is still a little scary, but the confidence I've gained in who God is for me is indescribable.

Don't allow the things you face on this journey to deter you from the purpose God has for you. I wouldn't dare tell you this is a cakewalk; instead, I'll say this is indeed a faith walk. However, the word of God says in John 16:33, "In this world, we will have trouble, but be of good cheer; God has overcome the world." If you find yourself feeling like you are in an uphill battle; look at it this way: you're simply building up your spiritual resume. After all, it's usually the most attractive resumes that are chosen. Embrace the lessons learned while on this journey with Christ. Build up your resume with the spiritual endeavors God wants to work in and through you. So again, I encourage you to trust the process.

Pray this prayer with me:
Father, in the name of Jesus, strengthen me for this journey. I understand I will not like everything I am faced with, but I promise to fall into Your arms instead of falling into old habits.

Help me trust You with the purpose You have placed on my life. Help me to remember You know the plans You have for me, and they are plans of good, and not evil. Continue to encourage my heart, as I go on this faith walk with You. Amen!

DAY 21

Queen of Busy
(Martha)
— Clarissa Pritchett —

"But Martha was distracted by all the preparations that had to be made. She came to him and asked, 'Lord, don't you care that my sister has left me to do the work by myself? Tell her to help me!'"
– Luke 10:40 (NIV)

MARTHA IS A woman in the Bible that could be my twin. In my opinion, Martha seemed like she was a woman who was always about the business, getting things done, and getting things done right. She also loved to serve others. She expected her sister to be like her and serve with the same heart. Martha was like most women who worry over the weight of responsibility they carry. She may have had a neverending "to do" list, and worked herself until she was weary. On the other hand, her sister Mary seemed to be able to live in the moment and relax. Martha also appeared to be a party planner and hostess. She invited everyone to the house and served them all. Martha and Mary were friends with Jesus. If I knew Jesus was going to come to one of my parties or events, I would have been working hard like Martha to make sure the whole house was clean and ready for him to arrive as a VIP guest.

Luke 10:38-42 it says, "A certain woman named Martha welcomed Him into her house. And she had a sister called Mary, who also sat at Jesus' feet and heard His word. But Martha was distracted with much serving, and she approached Him and said, 'Lord, do You not care that my sister has left me to serve alone? Therefore, tell her to help me." "And Jesus answered and said to her, 'Martha, Martha, you are worried and troubled about many things. But one thing is needed, and Mary has chosen that good part, which will not be taken away from her.'"

Martha may have felt like Mary was just leaving her to do all the work. Instead of causing drama or starting a fight, Martha took her frustrations straight to Jesus. She let Him know how she felt. He basically told her to calm down and chill. It seemed like Jesus gave Martha that gentle reminder that hearing His word was more important than all the work she was trying to get done.

Many times, when I'm overwhelmed, I can hear God reminding me that His word is more important than all the work I'm trying to get done too! I have been told I am the Queen of Busy. It really is a struggle for me to slow down. Have you ever seen the memes with the hashtag #GrowingUpHispanic on social media? Sis, let me tell you, sometimes I think growing up Hispanic gave me Obsessive Compulsive Disorder a.k.a. OCD. A trusted guide to mental health and wellness online says that a common sign of OCD is "ordering or arranging things "just so." I would not be surprised if you googled OCD and an old picture of me popped up. Growing up Hispanic as the oldest sibling of three, I had to have everything perfect in the house by the time my mom got home from work. I would get in trouble for not cleaning enough and get in trouble for not cleaning right.

By the time I was in kindergarten, my mom had me standing on a chair washing dishes. Lines had to be in the carpet after vacuuming with no footprints. My bed had to be made before I left for school in the morning. The bathroom had to be spic and span, and the air where we lived had to smell like Clorox, Pine Sole, or Fabuloso. If I did not fold my socks and underwear correctly and have the towels folded neatly, the clothes in my drawers would be dumped all over the floor when I got home from school to fold everything again "the right way." I had a fear of germs (I still don't like germs). I would get upset when my little sisters were not helping me and I felt like they were the ones who got to have all the fun playing outside while I was doing everything.

I never had issues in the military with passing room or uniform inspections because my mom prepared me as a child to always have things ready to inspect. As I grew into a young woman, these tendencies to have everything perfect turned me into the Queen of Busy. Even when I lived on my own, my apartment had to be organized and cleaned perfectly before I went to bed, left for class, or went to work. I only had myself to answer to, but I would still feel like I disappointed myself if things were not clean. That is crazy right? What is crazier is that I had thoughts like, "Lawd, if I die today, I can't have my apartment looking like a hot mess when people come over." My mentality was, "Let everything be done decently and in order." Being around disorganized people drove me nuts.

Eventually, I realized my tendencies were an issue. I asked God to help me relax. I meditated on Mathew 11:28 that says, " Come to me, all you who are weary and burdened, and I will give you rest." Over the years I did start to ease up. I started sleeping in, leaving the laundry to be imperfectly folded, leaving dirty dishes in the sink, and even watching T.V. while doing nothing else at the same time. Now as a "momma bear" of three boys, I can still sometimes feel my heart race when the house is a mess. Though I have gotten a lot better at not piling too much on my plate, I am still a work in progress. My hubby and close friends tell me I'm a busy bee. They say they worry about me taking on too much. I thank God for these reminders as it helps me take a step back and think about how I don't want my kids to have OCD like me. God blessed me with children, and I don't want them to get the tired worn-out version of me because I continue to be the Queen of Busy instead of being their mom.

So, sis, do you know God still loves you if you do not get things done and just right? Can you relax and pray to Him even when the dishes are not clean? Martha expected her sister to be helping her with everything when Jesus came to the house but Mary chose to sit at the feet of Jesus and hear His word. Jesus wants us to just sit and hear his word too!

God also wants the best of us in our prayer life instead of what is left of us after completing our "to do" list. He wants us to come to Him with our frustrations and take our expectations off of others to be busy like us. It is okay to admit we need help with our uptightness. God wants us to release the weight of the world we try to carry on our own so He can carry it for us. I believe our lives will be much healthier when we stop "the busy" together as women and simply sit with God and His word.

Pray this prayer with me
God, please help me give You the best of me instead of what is left of me. Help me start and end each day with You and keep You in the middle of everything I put my hands to do. Comfort me when anxiety rises and things are not perfect or left incomplete. Please do not let my "to do" list distract or keep me from reading Your word. Help me stop placing my expectations on others and getting disappointed when my expectations of others are not met. I thank You for loving me in my busyness. I also thank You for being there to carry the weight I put on myself. Please remind me to put You first and stay focused on what matters most.

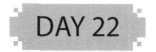

DAY 22

Sis, let it all go and let God deliver you!
(Mary Magdalene)
— Clarice May Cregger —

"Jesus said to the woman, your faith has saved you; go in peace..."
– (Luke 7:50 NIV)

THIS STORY IS about a woman in the bible named Mary Magdalene. Mary Magdalene is one of the most often mentioned women in the New Testament. Magdala is her place of birth. She is one of the most controversial figures in the bible. Mary was delivered from seven demonic spirits. After Jesus cast seven demons from her, Mary became one of his followers. She was very close to Jesus. Mary was the first to declare the good news that Jesus was raised from the dead. She is the one that saw a risen Christ first; she is the one the angel told that Jesus whom she was looking for was raised from the dead. This was an honor reserved for her – not the disciples. She bore witness to all the events that happened to Jesus leading up to his crucifixion and resurrection. Mary Magdalene is often associated with the woman caught in the act of adultery even though we do not know for sure if this was the same person the Pharisees and religious leaders wanted to stone. Mary suffered a lot because of demonic possession and oppression. The fact that seven demons lived in her could only mean that her life was in a horrible condition.

We all can relate to Mary's story. At one point in our lives, we were once what Mary was. We all have lived with sin. Some of us have lived with demonic oppression or possession before Jesus Christ delivered us. I know in my life I have struggled with my own bondages as well. The worrying spirit; the insanity of doing the same thing over and over while expecting different results. The most painful bondage I had to overcome was suicidal thoughts, and multiple attempts to hurt myself. I was in so much pain because of guilt, shame, and feeling alone. But God never gave up on me. He delivered me, just as Jesus delivered Mary Magdalene. He never gave up on her; he did not judge her because of her past. I learned that I had to completely let go, and let God take care of me. I had to understand the true love He really has for me. I had lost count of how many times God saved me. If we want to really change, it is our responsibility to seek Him first. Life will throw so many temptations and trials our way. We must stay grounded in His presence. Because if we do not, the enemy will use that opening (weakness) against us and try to come in to oppress us.

Suicide was the one thing I learned growing up. It was the action I thought would save me. But instead, it hurt me. I still remember how much I longed for the pain of hurting myself because that was the only thing that made me feel alive in a way. It is fascinating because I wanted the pain to feel alive but at the same time, I wanted to end it. But God loves us so much that he will do whatever it takes to grab hold of us. He will use circumstances and people in your life to show you how much he loves you. That even in the darkest time of your life you are never alone.

I want to encourage you, woman of faith, to not grow weary for His promise in your life is true. He knows the pain you are in. He knows your past, your present, and your future. He knows all the shame and guilt you have been carrying. He is just waiting for you to surrender. Surrendering to him is what saved me; saved me from my own self and the demons that were in me. So, if you are holding on to something dark and deep inside you because you feel ashamed, I encourage you to surrender, let go, let Him take care of you. And let Him release you from the bondages that are holding you back from what God called you to be.

Pray this prayer with me:

"God, I come to you as your humble servant asking that you release me from all the bondages in my life; show me the way to walk in freedom, Lord as you promise. "You have called me in righteousness, and you will also hold me by your hand and watch over me, And you will appoint me as a covenant to the people, As a light to the nations, To open blind eyes, To bring out prisoners from the dungeon And those who dwell in darkness from the prison..." (Isaiah 42:6-7) God, I pray that you use my story to edify and glory your name forever and ever. Amen.

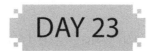

DAY 23

Birthing Purpose!
(Mary - Mother of Jesus)
— Rosie Thompson —

"Don't be afraid, Mary," the angel told her, "for you have found favor with God! You will conceive and give birth to a son, and you will name him Jesus. He will be very great and will be called the Son of the Most High. The Lord God will give him the throne of his ancestor David. And he will reign over Israel forever; his Kingdom will never end!"
– Luke 1:30-33

WHAT AN AMAZING story Mary, the mother of Jesus had! To be chosen for such a great calling. To be pregnant with a promise from God. To be told, "you have found favor with God"! She was expecting! Amazing, yes. But as some of us know, when a woman is expecting a child, it can be filled with pressure and discomfort. With a closer look at Mary's story, I began to see the pressure of carrying such a promise to full birth.

There can be much discomfort in carrying a promise. Having carried my own promises (and children), I imagined Mary had days where she questioned God. I imagined her trying to understand why God would choose someone like her. We all know He could've chosen anyone. She may have done like we often do when God calls us to do something great and questioned her qualifications and ability. Am I smart enough? Or wealthy enough? Will I be a good mother? She may have been misunderstood since she was not yet married. She may have been the talk of the town.

I began to question God. Why did You choose Mary? Was she a really good person? Was she that perfect child? I wanted to know how God decided that Mary would be the one to carry such a great promise. The angel did say to her in Luke 1:28 that she was, "well-favored among women". So, was she chosen because of her character? Maybe God knew He could trust her with this promise. Which led to my next question, "Lord, why did You choose me?" I wasn't well educated. I came from a background of abuse and molestation. I was so bruised and broken. I didn't feel favored at all. I felt shattered and like there was darkness all around me! Yet I have been chosen by God!

And now, I've been presented with this "baby" to birth which I feel like I've been with for a long time. I've been in labor waiting to bring forth the promise God placed inside of me. At times, there has been so much discomfort carrying the promise of God. It did not feel good at all. What I have learned is that in order to carry and then bring forth the promises of God, you must believe and know who you are in God. You also have to know your purpose. This is the answer I received from the Lord in response to my questions about Mary and myself. Mary knew her purpose. She understood the plan God had for her life. She knew that she was carrying the Messiah. Why? Because she believed the words of God spoken over her life.

Being inspired by Mary and taking a good look at myself, I decided that I was going to birth this promise. I am not running from the "birthing pains" and the restless nights anymore! I've begun to "push" with everything in me! With every groan and contraction in the Spirit, this baby is coming forth. Mary carried and birthed SALVATION for the world. And, like Mary, what I'm carrying and will bring forth by God's grace will bring many people into their purpose and plan for their lives.

There is a purpose for our pain. We must trust the process. He said he will never leave or forsake us. He lives inside of us no matter what we go through. So, women of God, our time of delivery has come. Let's bring forth His purpose!

Pray this prayer with me:
Father, I thank You for showing me Your awesome love and strength and for allowing me to walk in Your favor. I now know that greatness is on the inside of me to help hurting women whom I may come in contact with as I go through this life journey. Lord, thank you for being my shield and strength as I birth Your purpose through me. My heart trusts in You always. Amen

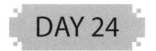

DAY 24

Chosen from Childhood
(Miriam, sister of Moses)
— Monique M. Moorer and Natalie A. Bryan —

"The baby's sister then stood at a distance, watching to see what would happen to him....Then the baby's sister approached the princess".
– (Exodus 2:4, 7a)

THERE ARE MOMENTS in life where we cannot understand the reason we are going through certain things. We try to mitigate why as a child we had to carry such responsibilities. The carefree life that we often long for did not seem to be for us. But, when we look back over our lives from an adult perspective, we can see how God has played an intricate part in every aspect of who we are. His hand has navigated our lives before we had full knowledge of who He is.

Miriam is first introduced in the bible in the second chapter of Exodus as an unnamed child. One who around the age of ten to twelve was given the task of watching over her infant brother, Moses, as their mother placed him in a waterproof basket to save his life. This is during the time when Pharaoh was killing the firstborn of the Hebrews for fear that their people would grow to outnumber the Egyptians. As the basket traveled across the Nile River, this young girl stood close by on the riverbank to oversee the fate of her brother.

As children of a single parent, we had to grow up very fast. We lived in a very economically challenged area of Brooklyn. We cooked, cleaned, and helped our younger siblings with homework. Without assistance, we learned how to instinctively navigate the hardened streets of our area as there was not and still to this day, is not a school bus to collect children from the corner to take to school. We maneuvered through crack vial paths and passed drunk people on the corner just to catch public transportation to get to school. We even assisted our mother in running multiple entrepreneurial businesses. Our vacations sometimes turned into work. By man's standard that would be too much for one of a tender age to handle, but by God's design, it was preparation for where He was taking us. The difficulties, hardships, and stereotypes we endured as children, molded us into successful and God-fearing women. God is so amazing that even in dark moments we may have felt abandoned or neglected by people, we never felt abandoned by Him. The humble beginnings did not stop the call that God had on each of us.

Both of us have become successful healthcare workers and have assisted our younger sisters in becoming successful public servants, the work did not stop there. There was a greater call which was to fulfill the Great Commission as Matthew 28:16-20 sets forth. Today we both function as licensed Ministers in the Body of Christ through our local ministry. Miriam was called to a greater office as well, the office of prophetess. And God has called you too. "You made all the delicate, inner parts of my body and knit me together in my mother's womb. Thank you for making me so wonderfully complex! Your workmanship is marvelous—how well I know it. You watched me as I was being formed in utter seclusion, as I was woven together in the dark of the womb. You saw me before I was born. Every day of my life was recorded in your book. Every moment was laid out before a single day had passed". (Psalms 139:13-16 NLT). He has need of your gift and talents. Although there were things that may have arisen when you were a child, God has created you for purpose. The task of Miriam watching over her brother preserved his life. All you need is a heart that is willing to do His will. (Psalms 57:2 ESV).

Miriam was willing to do the will of God. She was a bold child; bold enough to come from the bushes to approach Pharaoh's daughter and suggest their mother as a nurse for the child. That moment gave opportunity for their mother to instill the heritage of their people, the Israelites, in him. Our boldness as children should not be dimmed by the struggles of this life. Remember, we are not perfect, just striving to be Christ-like every day. God's word says, "dear children, do not let anyone lead you the wrong way. Christ is righteous. To be like Christ a person must do what is right". (1 John 3:7 NCV). Miriam had setbacks that resulted in serious consequences. But it did not mean that God did not love Miriam or use her. Her prophecies and prophetic songs were a great revelation of who God was to the children of Israel. Be bold for God. Though you may be young with great responsibilities, you have purpose and destiny and "can do all things through Christ who strengthens you". (Philippians 4:13. KJV).

Pray this prayer with me:

Father God, I thank you for all things that You have done for me. I thank You for the anointing that You have placed over my life and the grace You have given me. I ask that You continue to move and abound within me. I thank You for allowing me to be a blessing to others as You have blessed me! Lord continue to "open the floodgates of heaven and pour out so much blessing that there will not be room enough to store it". (Malachi 3:10 NIV). As You navigate my life through the Holy Spirit, continue to make and mold me as a potter does his clay. I thank You for making me an example for others. "Let the words of my mouth, and the meditation of my heart, be acceptable in thy sight, oh Lord my strength am my redeemer". (Psalms 19:14 KJV).

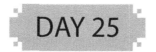

DAY 25

Never Underestimate New Beginnings
(Naomi)
— Deborah Rivers Decoteau —

'Don't call me Naomi, call me Mara, because
the Almighty has made my life very bitter."
– Ruth 1:20

NAOMI, THE ISRAELITE, was an alien in a strange land separated from the protection of God's law. Her family relocated from Bethlehem to Moab to escape a famine roughly 10 years earlier.

Naomi had reached an all-time low after the loss of her husband and her two sons. She felt like the hand of God was against her. She knew what becoming a widow meant. It meant her future would be difficult and dangerous. She had every reason to be scared.

We all have struggled with things. What happened to Naomi, could happen to us. I do not know what you are struggling with right now. My advice to you, is don't wait, run to the Lord in your struggle. Jesus can empathize with our struggles. Jesus wept. (John 11:35) He got angry (Matthew 21:12-13). He was rejected and abused, so he feels our pain.

I remember growing up as a child. When a loved one died the family kept the dead in the house (on ice, of course). Friends and neighbors would come by night after night to show their respect for the dead. The dead were dressed at the house and that is where the funeral procession would start until they got to the gravesite.

Death was very intimate. Today, the dead are kept in a funeral home and taken care of by strangers. I do not know what they did during Naomi's time but regardless, it can take a toll on your emotions.

My spiritual journey has had its share of peaks, valleys, and plateaus. I had to learn to "trust in the Lord with all my heart and lean not on my own understanding in all my ways. I had to acknowledge him and allow Him to direct my paths, Proverbs 3:5. I literally had to say this proverb every time I got anxious. There were times I did not have enough when I got paid to take care of my children and pay the bills. At times I went to bed with tears rolling down my cheeks because of the decisions I made that put me in the situation in which I found myself. There was no one to blame but myself. My only option was to stand on the promises of God and pray for my children to grow up quickly.

I know people like me are hurting every day. Sometimes, we have to take a moment and consider our struggles in life and remember how gracious and faithful God has been during those struggles and continue to trust and obey him. Remember, God is with you. He sees your struggles. Surrender and be still. He will take care of you better than you can take care of yourself.

There is help to be found during our storms in the word of God. Luke 18:1 says "At all times we ought to pray and not lose heart". Romans 5:3-5 tells us there is hope through the suffering, and David was pleading in Psalms 50:15 when he said "bring good from this bad situation". Deuteronomy 10:18 reminds us that God has a special place in his heart for widows.

Naomi and Ruth stuck together and genuinely took care of each other. Their relationship was favored by God. Ruth married a wealthy man, a kinsman of Naomi's. Through this union, Naomi was blessed, protected, and found renewed hope in her life.

Pray this prayer with me:
Holy one, may my security and strength come from you. Help

me to embrace the new seasons and change in my life. Give me wisdom and discernment to make decisions according to Your perfect will for my life. Amen

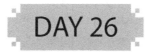

DAY 26

Sis, to be double-minded is to be Inconsistent
(Orpah)
— Clarice May Cregger —

"Their loyalty is divided between God and the world,
and they are Unstable in everything they do…"
– (James 1:8)

THIS STORY IS about a woman in the bible named Orpah who was from Moab. Orpah was the daughter-in-law of Naomi, the wife of Chilion. As we know from the Bible Moab was a pagan country with idolatrous practices. Naomi and her husband traveled to Moab to seek sustenance because of the famine their country was experiencing. Naomi and her husband never lost their faith in God, even in the midst of their hardship. Naomi's two sons both married Moabite women. One was named Ruth, and the other was Orpah. They all lived together harmoniously. Not long after, Naomi's husband and her two sons died, leaving them alone, poor, broken, and desolate. After the death of her husband and sons, Naomi decided to move back to her homeland. This meant Ruth and Orpah would have to choose whether or not to go with Naomi. They would have to leave the life they knew and in which they grew up. Naomi did not want to be selfish so she asked both women if they would like to join her. Ruth said yes; Orpah chose to stay behind in Moab.

Orpah's story is one to which all of us can relate. I remember being a young adult. The struggles to learn who you are at that age and where to go next are so prevalent. There is so much peer pressure to do certain things, be like somebody else, or dress a certain way; the list goes on. Orpah's story is so powerful. Even though she lost her husband God was there with her the entire time. He watched over her. God loves us so much that he would never leave us alone, although He gives us free will to choose who we want to be, to do whatever we want to do, and to choose to be born again. The question is what we are going to do with that gift of free will.

I made so many bad choices growing up. God said what you focus on and idolize becomes your god. This is very true in life. We often lose sight of our God-given purpose here on earth. We often fall into the traps this world has to offer. But God gives us grace every day; the grace to choose the right path and to rely on him with every decision we make. He is such a gentleman. He does not force us to choose Him, but He is there waiting and ready when we do choose Him. Sometimes we become like Orpah. We have a hard time letting go of the past.

I want to encourage you, woman of God. Remember, God delivered us from our sinful ways by sending his son Jesus Christ so that we can live our lives peacefully, full of joy and laughter. God wants us to move forward, not backward. We must remind ourselves that God has released and redeemed us from Egypt (our bondages), and we are to not go back. I wish I had learned this lesson a lot sooner when I was younger. I made so many double-minded decisions growing up that really pushed me away from my relationship with God.

In Matthew 5:37 God says, "All you need to say is simply 'Yes' or 'No'; anything beyond this comes from the evil one." We are to not be double-minded. To be double-minded is to be inconsistent, and untrustworthy. God wants us to live our life in full honesty and reliance on him.

Pray this prayer with me:
God, I come to you as your humble servant asking that where I lack wisdom, You give it to me. For you God, give generously to

all without reproach, I ask in faith, Lord without doubt, because the one who doubts is like a wave of the sea that is driven and tossed by the wind. For that person must not suppose that he will receive anything from You. (James 1:5-7) God, I pray against having a double mind. Amen.

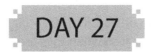

DAY 27

You will Thrive: Even in the Wilderness
(Priscilla)
— Robin Cuffee- King —

And found a certain Jew named Aquila, born in Pontus, lately come from Italy, with his wife Priscilla; (because that Claudius had commanded all Jews to depart from Rome:) and came unto them.
– (Acts 18:2)

PRISCILLA WAS A woman of power and authority. She is also noted as being loyal and generous. She and her husband are mentioned six times in the Bible because you will see that the two seemed inseparable. Together they were a powerhouse in the building of God's Kingdom. However, I really want you to know more about her and how many of us have been in the same shoes she wore.

In letters that the Apostle Paul wrote about Priscilla and her husband, he spoke highly of them. In Romans 16:3, Paul called them his helpers in Christ.

Priscilla's life journey was not easy. In fact, take a moment to visualize what I am about to write. Priscilla and her husband had been kicked out of their home country of Rome. They had to flee because all Jews were being expelled due to an edict that Emperor Claudius had issued.

I know during this time Priscilla had to feel hurt and abandoned by leadership. I know she and her husband must have had deep moments of sorrow to have to leave all that they had ever known and to go and build a new life elsewhere. But what I do believe is that even in this time of transition God pierced their hearts with His reassuring Word because when they arrived where God wanted them to be, the Apostle Paul sought them out. From this, a true testimony of discipleship developed.

Priscilla and her husband Aquila were so strong in faith that they were considered apostles by the Apostle Paul and were entrusted with an infant church he left behind. She was able to share God's Word. She and her husband were major contributors to the growth of Christianity in Corinth. They went on to have a church that was located in their home. This was a common practice in the home of prominent Christians of that time. Can you believe it? God had allowed them to prosper in what seemingly was a story that would end sooner or later in gloom.

I don't know about you but there have been so many times where I have been forced out of the comfort of home into a place that was new and strange. Even as I have felt overwhelmed with all the newness and unexpected challenges, my faith in God has always said, "no matter what you see, trust in me." So, I ask you, my sister, are you trusting God even if you feel like you are in the wilderness?

I know life circumstances are real; oftentimes, when we are forced into making changes we may not want or even agree with initially we may lack the faith to see it through. We may lack focus. We may lack discipline. There are so many things that we may lack but I believe that the God we serve will supply all of our needs according to HIS riches in glory. So even if you are in the wilderness and you feel as if you don't have enough, I am praying and decreeing that God's abundant blessings will overtake you.

Like Priscilla who had to leave all she had ever known, God stepped in and allowed her journey to become a testimony of His faithfulness to us. So, as you walk into your next level trust God because you WILL thrive.

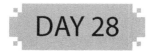

DAY 28

Rebuilding with Inspiration
(Proverb 31 Wife and Woman)
— Monique M. Moorer and Natalie A. Bryan —

"There are many virtuous and capable women in the world,
but you surpass them all"!
– (Proverbs 31:29 NLT)

DO YOU KNOW that you surpass all of the virtuous and capable women in the world? Do you believe it? Well, guess what? God's word says so. For all women especially those that are preparing to be wives, God shows us in His word that our potential in life is far beyond anything that we could think or imagine. He has made us with grace and strength, sympathy, and empathy. We are creative and innovative. We are complex beings created in His image. All we have to do is tap into all that he has placed inside of us. Although the text takes place in a time where wives mainly covered the children and the home while the husbands worked outside the home, it still applies today. God gives clear and concise instructions on how we should dress, speak, deal with our family, and reverence Him.

Growing up in a household of only women, the line that established the characteristic differences between men and women got blurred very easily. As young ladies, we did everything that needed to be done in the home. We cleaned the house, we cooked the food, we learned to comb hair, hem clothing, and cared for our younger sibling; just to name a few. We also had part-time jobs, went to school and obtained good grades, and covered the family businesses. Yes, there was more than one. Where verse 16 says "she goes to inspect a field and buys it; with her earnings she plants vineyards", that was my family of women. This was all before we were eighteen. We later dealt in real estate as well as other entrepreneurial ventures. But, preparing for, and entering into marriage was something new. It was foreign. We knew that it was something we desired. Our imaginations pictured one thing, but the reality was truly different. Life became confusing and difficult trying to navigate it from a new perspective.

Learning to do everything on your own can make the transition to marriage very hard. Where does being raised as a strong, independent woman fit into a partnership? This question reigns loud and true, especially if you are married to a man that knows the godly meaning of "head of household." There was complete evidence that I misunderstood the real definition of "the two becoming one." Having my own money and doing my own thing was what I was taught to do. Marriage is a new concept for many of us, therefore, we need to know how to navigate this new venture. God's word is amazing! He constantly reminds us of who we are. He tells us who we are. "For we know, brothers and sisters loved by God, that he has chosen you". (1 Thes 1:4 NIV). We are His chosen ones. He is constantly reminding us that we are strong in Him. "I love you, Lord, my strength. The Lord is my rock, my fortress, and my deliverer". (Psalm 18:1 NIV).

For a long time, I questioned my worthiness of marriage. I even questioned if this path is what God purposed for me to do. He made it clear that His answer was yes. This meant I now had to look at myself the way that God saw me, and sees me in every moment, as enough. No more putting myself down or feeling like I was less than. Although Natalie's marriage ended in divorce, my marriage is still in progress and it requires work. After major transitions occur, the next step is rebuilding.

Let us all rebuild. Encourage yourself. Since "faith comes by hearing and hearing by the word of God" Romans 10:27 (KJV), let us declare Proverbs 31 over our lives. Let God's word inspire you to be free in Him. Know who God has called you to be. You are more precious than rubies. You shall greatly enrich your husband's (husband-to-be's) life. You will make great business decisions. You will dress in fine clothing. You are strong and dignified. You are wise and work hard. You are blessed by your children (natural or spiritual). You have joy. You will be praised by your husband. You will be rewarded publicly for all that you have done. You see, all of these affirmations are the way that God sees you. With a new perspective of you, God's masterpiece; the Proverbs 31 woman, walk fully in the confidence of who you are as a single woman, a woman in waiting, or a wife. You surpass all others because God said so.

Pray this prayer with me:

Heavenly Father, I thank you for who you are in my life. I thank you for the blessings you have bestowed upon me. I thank you for everything that I have experienced as it has drawn me closer to you. I am grateful that you have called me before I was formed in my mother's womb. I know that I am a daughter of the King and Most High and that I am fearfully and wonderfully made. As a Proverbs 31 woman, my worth is far more than rubies. I am confident that when my enemies try to come in like a flood, You will lift up a standard against them. I have a future filled with hope. I know that You, God, are intentional about my life. Lord continue to hide me in Your secret place. I thank you for blessing me with the peace that surpasses all understanding as I realize no matter what I go through, Your glory will be revealed in my life. I thank you and praise you. In Jesus' name. Amen.

DAY 29

Sis, Obedience, Patience, Faith, and Loyalty Go a Long Way
(Rachel)
— Clarice May Cregger —

"Thus, says the Lord: Refrain your voice from weeping, and your eyes from tears; for your work shall be rewarded, says the lord, and they shall come back from the land of the enemy."
– (Jeremiah 31:16)

THIS STORY IS about a woman in the bible named Rachel. Rachel was one of Laban's daughters. She was sister to Leah and second wife to Jacob. Jacob was running away from his brother because he had deceived his brother from his blessing. Jacob's parents told him to go to Haran and live with his mother, Rebecca's brother, Laban. He saw Rachel at the well and immediately fell in love with her. Rachel was "lovely in form and beautiful," the Bible says. He then later met Rachel's father Laban and promised to work for him for 7 years with no pay in exchange for Rachel's hand in marriage which is Rachel. After serving Laban for seven years, Jacob was ready to marry Rachel as promised by Laban. On the night of the wedding, he thought he was laying next to Rachel. The next morning, he discovered it was her older sister, Leah. Laban had betrayed Jacob. Both Jacob and Rachel were devastated but that did not stop Jacob. He served another seven years and finally was able to marry Rachel.

Leah gave birth to many sons and daughters for Jacob. But because Rachel was favored and loved, God made her barren. In her desperation for children, Rachel gave her handmaiden to lay with Jacob, and she too gave birth to an heir to Jacob. God was not deaf, nor blind to Rachel's pain. After several years, God allowed Rachel to get pregnant and she gave birth to her first son, Joseph.

It was many years before Rachel was able to bare a child again. But even in the middle of her reproach God never forsook her. God saw how faithful, loyal, and obedient she was to him, and to her husband Jacob. So, God blessed her with another son named Benjamin, although this pregnancy cost her life. Jacob had 12 sons between Leah, her maid, and Rachel and her maid. All 12 of his sons were heads of the tribe of families that became the nation of Israel.

The story of Jacob and Rachel shows all of us how much God loves us. Think of Jacob's unwavering love for Rachel and his willingness to serve Laban for seven years. It shows his obedience, patience, and love. Imagine God, and how long He sometimes waits for us to come to Him. Rachels' story reminds me of a time in my life when I felt so unloved, unwanted, and hopeless. I lost my identity. I lost my desire to have children of my own. As a woman, the pressure of having everything together was like a goal. I focused so much on just being a wife to my husband and a hard-working citizen. Nothing else mattered to me. I did not make friends. I did not have any aspirations. I did not have any dreams or goals. I even lost faith in my relationship with God. My husband and I got married at such a young age. I was only 19 years old. I did not know any better. I was so young and careless. I became so codependent on my husband and lost sight of who God was, and my calling in life. I went through such a traumatic experience during my early to late teenage years and that built my perspective of life. All I wanted was a sense of normalcy, even if that meant losing my identity.

I had been married for seven years when my husband and I separated. I had hit rock bottom; I was a mess. I finally admitted to myself that I had lost sight of who I was. I had tried hard to conform to societal norms – get married and have children.

During our separation, just like Rachel weeping to God, I asked God why this was happening to me? All I wanted was to have a family. I just wanted to be loved, to love my husband, and our future children. I realized that everything was not in my timing. God had a purpose for every pain Rachel experienced. And just like Rachel, God has a purpose for every pain that we experience. My husband and I were separated for two years. At that time, I learned so much about myself and God. I know that God loves us so much; He just wants the best for us. Even if that means a temporary heartbreak. God said He is close to the broken-hearted. He had to remove my husband from the picture so that He could have all of me, and so He could work on me. God taught me patience, obedience, and loyalty in that season so that when He brought my husband back, I could be the wife God intended me to be for him.

I want to encourage you, woman of God, to believe in your heart that God sees you and hears you. He loves you so much that He is willing to see you go through the pain and be with you through it all, just to see you grow. Sometimes we get angry because we do not have what we thought we should by now. For me that is children, But I know God has a plan and that plan is better than what I have in store for me. So, do not lose faith, stay obedient, and know the best is yet to come.

Pray this prayer with me:

God, I come to You as Your daughter, asking You to help me, be on guard, to stand firm in my faith, to be courageous, and to be strong. (1 Corinthians 16:13:) God, I thank You for the grace bestowed upon me and the unconditional love You have for me even when I feel I don't deserve it. Keep me close to you and show me the way so that I may grow to be the woman You have called me to be. Amen.

DAY 30

Using your Faith to Unlock God's Favor
(Rahab, The Harlot)
— Patti Denise Henry —

"So the young men who had been spies went in and brought out
Rahab and her father and mother and her brothers and all who
belonged to her. And they brought all her relatives and put them
outside the camp of Israel."
– Joshua 6:23

RAHAB, THE HARLOT was born in the walled city of Jericho in the
land of Canaan. She was born to pagan parents, in a pagan society
with no belief in a monotheistic God. Jericho was known for being
the oldest city in biblical history. It is also known as the place where
the walls fell down when Joshua and the army of Israel captured the
city, with the help of God.

Rahab lived in a home that would be considered prime real
estate as it was located near the gates of the city and built into the
city walls. She was very easy to find by the men entering and leaving
her city. People knew who she was not only because of how she
earned her living but because of where she lived. This distinguished
her from other women who earned a living in the same manner;
after all, Jericho was a large city. Rahab was consistent in her craft.
No matter where her name was spoken it was accompanied by
what she did. Rahab the Harlot, the Prostitute, the Hooker, no last
name needed.

How is it, you may ask, that the Creator of the universe, the
Alpha and the Omega, our Father God would have a heart for

someone like her? To be fair, I would like to share some of her unmentioned attributes that I found to be attractive despite the fact that she sold sex for a living.

Rahab possessed wisdom, understanding, insight, bravery, courage, kindness, and leadership. She had the ability to negotiate, had geographical awareness, was the keeper of secrets, and knew the power and majesty of the God of the Israelites. She had faith in God. The fragrance of her faith reached the nostrils and heart of God. This type of faith was so attractive to God that He made a covenant to protect her and her entire family when Joshua and his army of soldiers returned to destroy her entire city.

Like Rahab, there was a time in my life when others judged me for choices. I got caught up in one wrong relationship after another. I had such an insatiable appetite to be loved and accepted that I found myself in a series of disappointing and embarrassing conditions. Oh, but God! He looked past my sin, shame, disgrace, guilt, and fear! He heard my cry for help and as He did with Rahab, He made a covenant with me after I voiced my belief and acceptance of Him. I placed my faith in His promises to love me and deliver me from the painful regrets of my past.

How does your faith stand up in times of trouble? What are you willing to chance and/or change in order to walk away from your sinful past, your mistakes, addictions, and habitual errors?

Beloved, God has a heart for you. A heart full of tender mercies, loving kindness, acceptance, and grace. God is bigger than your past and current problems, bigger than your sins, bigger than your pre-planned destiny. Will you exercise enough faith to not only believe but to declare your desire to have Him as your covering?

Rahab made a decision to choose God and His people over her own. She believed in this God. She confessed to the spies who God was. His favor and His heart for her allowed Him to overlook her name, her occupation, her livelihood, and her lies, and make a lasting covenant to protect her. This is a beautiful example to let you know that the heart of God is filled with forgiveness and provision for your future no matter what your past mistakes were.

Hebrews 11:31 "By faith, Rahab the Harlot, did not perish with those who were disobedient, because she had given a friendly welcome to the spies."

In future studies, we are told that Rahab, the Harlot, after Jericho was destroyed, moved to Israel where she met a man named Salmon, who built the city of Bethlehem. Rahab married Salmon and was the mother of Boaz, who married Ruth, who was the mother of Obed who was the father of Jesse, who was the father of King David from whom Jesus the Christ descended. Yes. Rahab, the Harlot is in the genealogy of Jesus Christ simply because she had faith, and God had a heart for her. Your past does not predict the outcome of your future!

Matthew 1:5 "And Salmon, the father of Boaz, by Rahab and Boaz the father of Obed, by Ruth, and Obed, the father of Jesse."

Affirmation: By God's grace I have a bright future and I am not defined by the sins of my past.

Pray this prayer with me:

Father, I approach You in the name of Your son Jesus. I accept and acknowledge that because of His death, burial, and resurrection that the wages for my sins were paid in full. I accept that He presents me as faultless and upon that cross He took away all of the guilt and all of the shame associated with the mistakes of my past, present, and future. I thank You, dear God, for creating me with a purpose and with a plan which will be fulfilled in my life. Father, I have enough faith and experience to believe that You are the one true living God, and I will shout it from the rooftop even in the presence of my enemies. Thank you for coming to my rescue. Amen

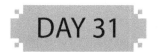

DAY 31

God's Purpose Will Prevail!
(Rebekah)
— Jessica Jená Green —

"And not only that, but Rebekah conceived children through one man, our father Isaac. 11 For though her sons had not been born yet or done anything good or bad, so that God's purpose according to election might stand— 12 not from works but from the one who calls—she was told, The older will serve the younger."
– Romans 9:10-12CSB

REBEKAH WAS THE great-niece of Abraham. and the sister of Laban. Rebekah became the wife of Isaac, who was the son that God promised to Abraham and Sarah. Rebekah bore two sons, Esau and Jacob. Rebekah's story is special because it is a good reminder that no matter what our mistakes may be, God can still use us. God's purpose for our life can prevail and WILL prevail. "This message shows that God chooses people according to his own purposes; he calls people, but not according to their good or bad works." Romans 9:11-12.

Sometimes we attempt to cancel ourselves along with our purpose because of the things that we have done in our past. Rebekah didn't do everything the right way. She and Isaac at one point lied about her being his wife. She even manipulated her husband so that her younger son Jacob could get the double portion blessing to which the firstborn son, Esau, was entitled. Although she did bad things, she still played a significant role in the bible.

Like Rebekah, we all have done things of which we aren't proud. But today, I want you to remember that God knows who you were, who you are, and who you are becoming. However, the beautiful thing is that who you were can't cancel out who you are BECOMING. Don't let anyone (not even yourself) limit you to your past because it doesn't stop God from moving in your present nor your future. God knew you before you knew you, and before the world knew you!

Today, accept that God chooses you not according to your good or bad works but the plans he had for you before you were conceived in your mother's womb. Say it out loud and boldly sis: "God has a purpose and a plan for me and my life!" Sis, God can and will use you in spite of what was meant to cancel you out. Your calling is bigger than your past. Your purpose is bigger than your past! Walk in that truth, today sis!

Pray this Prayer with Me:
God, please forgive me for running from the call on my life. Forgive me for running away from purpose due to my own insecurities about my past. Today, I say yes Lord! Yes to your will and yes to your way, daddy! Thank you, God, for having plans for me; plans to prosper me and plans for a hopeful future. (Jeremiah 29:11). I declare and decree that you are equipping me with everything that I need to do your will, Lord. In spite of my past, I have the right godly communities, the right resources, the ideas, the guidance, and the wisdom that I need. God, please continue to produce in me, every good thing that is pleasing to you through the power of Jesus Christ. All the glory to you forever Lord. (Hebrews 13: 20) In Jesus' name I pray, Amen.

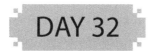

DAY 32

Sister You Are Not Mistaken
(Rhoda)
— Min. Vickey Neal —

Then I heard the voice of the Lord saying, whom shall I send, and
who will go for us then I said here am I. Send me!
– (Isaiah 6:8)

Today if ye will hear his voice, harden not your hearts, as in the
provocation.
– (Hebrews 3:15)

RHODA WAS LIVING in the house of Mary, who is the mother of John
Mark. Rhoda was the maidservant. Many people gathered there at
the house that night to pray for Peter. Rhoda was sitting in the back
of the room near the back door. There was unceasing prayer for Peter.
Peter had been cast into prison by King Herod and was in imminent
danger of death. Because of the prayers of the saints, Peter was
freed by an angel from prison. Rhoda was pretty much at the age
to establish her faith. She sat with her head bowed while mother
Mary was praying for Peter in the upper room. A knock sounded at
the door. She was so overjoyed when she heard Peter's voice that
she forgot to let him in. Rhoda was the first to hear the knock. She
ran to the upper room to let Mary know that their prayers had been
answered and Peter was standing at the door. Mary told her that she
was mistaken and out of her mind. Rhoda kept insisting that it was
Peter at the door. They said to her "it must be Peter's angel". Peter
knocked louder. When Mary opened the door, they saw Peter.

Even though Rhoda was a maidservant she was in a good position. She wasn't being distracted with the duties that she'd have to do later or the duties that were present before her. I am sure that Rhoda was praying and in agreement with the prayers about Peter being released from prison because she became overjoyed when she heard the voice of Peter. Therefore that place that she was in she had to be in position or she would have missed the signature knock that alerted her that the prayers of the righteous had been answered.

Sis, this story is very special to me because when it comes to the voice of God it is very important that there be no noise. What I mean by noise is clutter, holding on to the past; too busy for God; being a busybody in someone else's life. I'm in a leadership position and it's very important that I be in position to hear God's voice just like Rhoda heard Peter's knock at the door. So, I have to be in position when the people are praying for a move of God or a word from God. I have to be able to hear what God is saying and deliver his word to his people.

Sis, humbling yourself before God is a great place to start so he can speak to your heart and spirit. It's very hard to have a proud and arrogant spirit and hear God. Jeremiah 33:3 reads "Call to me and I will answer you, and I will tell you great and hidden things that you have not known." We have to be in a place to hear God. He is waiting to talk to you. God has secrets that he wants to share with you.

"I will instruct you and teach you in the way you should go; I will counsel you with my eye upon you. Be not like a horse or mule without understanding, which must be curbed with bit and bridle, or it will not stay near you." (Psalms 32:8-9) This is God's way of saying that he has a plan for your life. The plan that He has for you is, "plans to prosper you and not harm you, plans to give hope and a future." It is very easy, sister, to be misled if you're not seeking the will of God. It's important that you find your place in his presence, humbling yourself so he can guide you in every step of this journey. His word is true. (Deuteronomy 31:6) "Be strong and courageous; do not be afraid or terrified because of them, for the Lord your God goes with you he will never leave you nor forsake you."

Pray this prayer with Me

Father, I ask you to give me a complete understanding of what you want me to do in my life. I will always honor and please you. I will continually do good, kind things for others, while I seek your face. I ask you this day to unclutter my life and take everything that's not like you away from me. I dedicate myself and my time to your word. I believe your word is true. I put all of my trust in you. Amen.

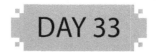

DAY 33

Genuine Christian Love
(Ruth)
— Deborah Rivers Decoteau —

"Intreat me not to leave thee. Where thou goest I will go; where
thou lodgest I will lodge and thy people shall be my people and
thy GOD my GOD. Where thou diest will I die and there will I be
buried. The Lord do so to me and more also, if ought but death
part thee and me.
– (Ruth 1:16-17)

AFTER THE DEATH of her husband, Ruth was given the opportunity
to return to her mother's house. Her mother-in-law, Naomi, was
headed back to her home and her people. The words that came out
of Ruth's mouth through her tears was not what Naomi expected.
"Intreat me not to leave thee, where you go, I will go; where you lay,
I will lay and your people shall be my people, and your God my God.
Where you die will I die. Only death will separate us. (Ruth 1:13). That
was the beginning of a very special relationship.

Ruth showed great courage when she decided to make that
long journey into a foreign land leaving all the customs she knew
behind. I believe that Ruth needed Naomi just as much as Naomi
needed her. They would be better together to comfort, support,
and help each other heal. Ruth had youth on her side and Naomi
had wisdom and her GOD to sustain her.

Sometimes circumstances and situations happen in our lives
that we cannot understand or explain but we must continue to trust

in the Lord. As believers, we sometimes fail at this, but he is forever faithful.

Like many believers, I too find myself experiencing some of those same fleshly emotions during my valley experiences. At a very young age, I experienced what felt like the wrath of GOD on my life. Nine months into my marriage, and two months after the birth of my first child, I almost lost my husband in a car accident. That experience changed my life forever. In the twinkling of an eye, I became the head of the household. I was forced into finding a job, transportation, and somewhere to live. By the grace of GOD, I did it! I can safely say from that moment He has been carrying me. He makes a way where there seems no way. I love that about my GOD!

My personal journey has led me down several difficult and sometimes dangerous roads, during which times, I turn to the Word of God and lean on His promises. "I will never leave you nor forsake you", has been one of my favorite promises. This familiar verse can be found in several places in the bible. We do not know the plans GOD has for us, but if we believe in His word and feed ourselves on His word every day, we can rest assured He is going to work everything out for His glory and edification. He continues to do that in my life even today. God hears and answers prayers in His own time. My advice is to be still and know that He is God. Psalms 46:10.

Ruth's loyalty and commitment to Naomi was ordained by the hand of GOD. In the end, Ruth marries Boaz, kinsman to Naomi's dead husband. God blesses them with a son, Obed who was the father of Jessie and Jessie was the father of King David. They all played a vital role in the genealogy of Jesus Christ. BE ENCOURAGED.

Pray this prayer with me
Father God, teach me to draw close to you for strength and wisdom and to praise you when things are going well and when they are not! Through Jesus Christ, I pray. Amen!

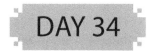

DAY 34

Don't Laugh At The Promise
(Sarah)
— Brittaney Pleasant —

"So, she laughed silently to herself and said, "How could a worn-out woman like me enjoy such pleasure, especially when my master— my husband-is also so old? Then the Lord said to Abraham, "Why did Sarah laugh? Why did she say, 'Can an old woman like me have a baby?' Is anything too hard for the Lord? I will return about this time next year, and Sarah will have a son."
— Genesis 18:12-13 NLT

ONE OF THE most beautiful attributes of God is His ability to keep His promises. There are several instances in the Bible where He made promises to His children. One example is Sarah, the wife of Abraham. Because she was barren, Sarah did not believe God when he told her she would conceive and bear a son. As if being barren for so many years wasn't enough of a reason for Sarah to be in disbelief, she was also almost 90 years old when God made this promise to her. Have you ever received a promise so far from your current reality that you could not believe it would ever come true? I think this is exactly how Sarah felt. In fact, the promise seemed so impossible that she laughed at God.

Although it seems like a big "no-no," to doubt, let alone laugh at God, I cannot say I blame Sarah. Considering her circumstances, it's easy to understand her disbelief. That is unless you have come to truly know and understand God and His power. In the not so distant past, I remember feeling so defeated. I had just given birth to my first child and filed for divorce. I was anxious, depressed, terrified of my future as a single mother, and I felt so alone. It wasn't the life that I envisioned for myself. I could not understand why I couldn't have my "happily ever after." In the midst of my fear and my pain, God spoke to me and said that redemption would be my portion and He would give me beauty for ashes. Sis, as beautiful as it sounded I was low-key rolling my eyes and saying, "yeah, right," under my breath. I wouldn't even give myself permission to believe it because it just seemed so far from the mess my life had become. I couldn't see how it was possible. But God! I am so very glad that His ability and willingness to keep his promises is not contingent upon our belief. Even though Sarah laughed at God, He still kept His promise, blessed her womb and allowed her to conceive and give birth to a son in her old age. Even though I was so unbelieving, God did, and is continuing to redeem me and is constantly making my life more beautiful as the days go by. I went from being divorced to being a single mother, to being loved deeply by, and married to a God-fearing man. My story is not over, sis, and neither is yours. Never allow your current circumstances to cause you to laugh at the promises of God. You are never so far from Him that He can't reach down, pick you up, and change your life.

Pray this prayer with me:
Father God, I come before You asking You to help me to know that nothing can separate me from Your love. Show me that every promise that You speak over me shall come to pass for You are not a man that You should lie. When I am unsure, help me to acknowledge You in all my ways so that You can direct my path. In Jesus name, I pray, amen.

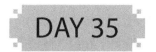

DAY 35

Restoration is Yours!
(The Shunamite Woman)
— Rosie Thompson —

Then he lay down on the child's body, placing his mouth on the child's mouth, his eyes on the child's eyes, and his hands on the child's hands. And as he stretched out on him, the child's body began to grow warm again! Elisha got up, walked back and forth across the room once, and then stretched himself out again on the child. This time the boy sneezed seven times and opened his eyes!
– 2 Kings 4:34-35

LOOK INTO THE eyes of the Shunammite woman and you will find courage. She was wealthy and generous as we learn from the manner in which she offered the prophet Elisha food as he traveled back and forth on his journeys. She and her husband even built and furnished a small room for him on their roof so that he would have a place to rest when he stopped by. One day, reflecting on their generosity Elisha inquired of what he could do to return the favor. She declined the favor insisting that her family took good care of her. But like God, who sees more for us than we see for ourselves, Elisha decided she should be blessed with a son. Enter the promise of God: "Next year at this time you will be holding a son in your arms!" 2 Kings 4:16. And she did!

Can you imagine the planning and the joy at the baby's arrival? Imagine the anticipation and the talks with her friends and family. Imagine the gratitude in her heart towards God for such an amazing blessing. Imagine holding Baby for the first time, first steps, first words, and the like. Then imagine it all come crashing down. Have you ever had something you were excited to receive be snatched away from you in the blink of an eye? Have you ever lost anything or anyone dear to you? Well, this is part of the Shunammite woman's story. Her promised child suddenly began to complain of head pain and soon after died in her lap. What do you do when you lose the promise and through no fault of your own?

Most of us would panic, mourn, ask "Why me, God?" Some of us would fall out with God and become angry with the man of God for getting our hopes up just to be let down. But the Shunammite woman was not like most of us in this situation. After realizing that she had lost her son, "she carried him up and laid him on the bed of the man of God, then shut the door and left him there." Kings 4:21 Then, without even telling her husband of the boy's condition, she hurried to Elisha the prophet. Elisha's servant asked her if everything was ok and she replied, "all is well." Elisha, though, could sense something was troubling her. Thank God for the people in our lives that can hear our silence; who can see the pain in our eyes; who will seek God on our behalf.

She said as many of us say, Lord, I didn't ask for this. I didn't ask to get my hopes up just to be let down. Elisha immediately understood that something was wrong with her promised child. And with that, he sprang into action to rectify the situation. Sometimes it's like that with God. Even though it may not be immediately noticeable, when we cry out to Him, He will spring into immediate action. Isaiah 65:24 tells us this: "I will answer them before they even call to me. While they are still talking about their needs, I will go ahead and answer their prayers!"

When Elisha arrived, he was able to revive her son. Her promise was restored. God breathed life back into her son. In the same manner, He can and will breathe life into some of our dead situations. Your promise may not be lost. Your marriage may not be lost. Your children may not be lost. Your business may not be lost. It may just need a touch from our Heavenly Father!

I'm learning when my life gets complicated, feels hopeless, and it seems like my back is against the wall, the best thing to say is, "all is well!" Those simple three words soothe my doubts and calm my fears. They keep me from trying to figure out my situation. They give me the peace to just leave it in God's hands to let Him handle it. Maybe you are like the Shunammite woman and me and have had promises just die in your lap. Some promises you asked for and some you didn't. And while you were gratefully enjoying them, they just died. I implore you to choose not to panic and instead go to God. Let Him restore every dead situation in your life as only he can.

Pray this prayer with me

Father, I thank you for being the restorer of my life. You repair all the broken places and bring life to every dead situation according to Your perfect will. Just like it says in Hebrews 11:35, the "women received their loved ones back again from death." Well, Father, I lay before You every dead thing that You wish to make live again. Restore me, oh God! Return unto me all the years stolen from me. Restore all the love I've given out and refill my cup so that it can run over yet again. In Jesus name, I pray. Amen! And it is so!

DAY 36

You Are Gifted Sis, and You Are A Giver
(Tabitha AKA Dorcas) Acts 9:36-42
— Min. Vickey Neal —

Then Peter arose and went with them. When he was come, they
brought him into the upper chamber: and all the widows stood by
him weeping, and shewing the coats and garments which Dorcas
made, while she was with them.
– Acts 9:39

THE BIBLE REMINDS us to stir up the gift of God which is in us
through the laying on of our hands (2 Timothy 1:16). The Bible also
speaks whoever sows sparingly will also reap sparingly and if you
sow generously will also reap generously 2 Corinthians 9:6

Tabitha, also called Dorcas, was a compassionate and devout
woman from a city named Joppa. She was a woman that was led
and taught by God. Tabitha was known for her good works and the
acts of charity she had shown to everyone with whom she came in
contact. Tabitha had great compassion for the widows in that city.
She was a very generous person and kind-hearted. God had given
her the gift of sewing and she used her gift to make clothes for the
needy. She would also sew for whoever asked of her. Tabitha also
had the gift of love. She willingly gave of her time.

One day Tabitha became ill and passed away. She was cleaned
up and taken into an upper room. Everyone that heard of Tabitha's
death was saddened. They just couldn't understand how a woman

with such gifts and good deeds could be taken away. All they had of her was memories. So, the people of Joppa dispatched some men to the next town, called Lydda, to find Peter, tell him what happened, and ask him to come pray for Tabitha. When Peter heard the message, he went to the city of Joppa. He entered the room where Tabitha was lying. Peter prayed to God. After his prayer, he turned to her and said "Tabitha arise". Tabitha rose up and was well. For all her good works God saw fit to heal her. After seeing that miracle many people became followers of Christ because God miraculously restored her life.

Sis, I have so much in common with Tabitha. I'm a woman that's seeking after God's own heart, being led and taught by Him. When I made the choice to accept him as my Lord and Savior, I knew that I was to serve him and his people. The gifts of God started to manifest in my life even more as I continued to dedicate myself to him. I found myself giving to those in need. The more I followed the Lord I had nothing but love for his people. I may not have the gift of a seamstress, but when God stirred up the gift on the inside of me he showed me that I had the gift of love.

I didn't understand that I love to hug people. It felt good to just love on people. One day during one of our church services in prayer time my pastor came and told me to go and hug this young lady that was up there for prayer. She had not told him what she wanted prayer for, but God knew what was on her heart. Once I wrapped my arms around her the young lady began to weep uncontrollably and fell to the floor. I laid there with her with my arms still wrapped around her. After the service, the young lady was asked to have words. She began to say how free she felt. She said, "I was feeling suicidal and not feeling loved, but when the sister put her arms around me it felt like Jesus was hugging me". I began to cry tears of joy.

There was a time in my life where I had to go through some things. It felt to me as though I had died spiritually. I wasn't effective to the body of Christ like I should have been because I was being made to endure more things in my life. I thank God for the people that felt that I was going through because at that point they started to pray for me and my strength. As I felt the prayers of the people, the spirit of God began to strengthen my life. I am stronger than ever. For that reason, I'll forever be thankful to God. I will do whatever he is calling me to do because I am grateful to be able to love on his people again.

Sis, I am convinced that God created man out of love. Even now I think about the verse, "For God so loved the world that he gave his only begotten son" (John 3:16). Sis, that's real love. To give your son up to die for others' sins, what greater love is that? Once we receive the spirit of God we become a giver of ourselves. We die to our flesh. We deny ourselves, pick up our cross, and follow him and leave everything else behind. Then the obedience of God will be our ultimate sacrifice. (1 John 4:8 (NLT) "But anyone who does not love does not know God, for God is love."

Sis, with all those gifts on the inside of you there's nothing that you can't do. You are going to do marvelous things through Christ. If you haven't already, I encourage you to accept him as your Lord and savior today. You too can make a difference.

Pray this prayer with me:

Heavenly Father, I am a firm believer in Your word. I know that I can do all things through Christ who strengthens me. I will trust You to lead me and guide me in all truth. I know that You will never leave me nor forsake me. I know that if I trust in You, I will not fear anyone or anything. For those reasons, I put all my trust in You. This day and every day I will accept You as my Lord and Savior Jesus Christ. (John 14:6) Amen

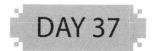

DAY 37

Move out the way!
(Tamar)
— Brejette Terry-Emery —

"For God is not a God of disorder but of peace as in all the
congregations of the Lord's people."
– 1 Corinthians 14:33

THE WOMAN OF the bible we will cover here is Tamar. Tamar was
promised to Judah's first-born son Er. Er's life was ended early by
God because of his wickedness. Tamar was then given to Judah's
second-born son Onan. Onan refused to have a child with Tamar for
he knew the child would proceed him as an heir. Onan made sure
to do everything possible to not impregnate Tamar. God was not
pleased, and also took the life of Onan. Judah had a third son but in
fear that he would also die, he refused to give Tamar to him. He tells
Tamar to return to her father's home until his son Shelah is of age.
Later Judahs' wife passes away, making Judah a widower. Judah
returns to Timnath to tend to his land. When Tamar hears that he is
coming, and understands that he is not going to keep his promise
of allowing his third son, Shelah, to marry her, she covers herself
with a veil and poses as a prostitute to meet Judah. Judah asks her
to lay with him in return for a baby goat. Tamar does and becomes
pregnant with twins Perez and Zerah. When Judah finds out that
Tamar is pregnant, he demands that Tamar be put to death until he
learns that the children are his. He allows Tamar to live because he
sees she was more righteous than him, in that he had not kept his
promise to marry his son to her.

As with the many promises to Tamar, I am reminded of a time in my life at the age of 27. I was recently separated after an 11-year relationship, I had lost my father, and it appeared that many things were happening to bring me down. At this time, I had been promised multiple positions and raises. Each time that I completed the tasks required, the goals were pushed farther and farther back so that I might never be able to attain the goal. I begged God for change and for the opportunity to be a supervisor or manager as I felt my talents would be better served. Soon after that prayer, I was offered a management position. It would appear that I would have the authority over many departments, but I would not be able to have a voice and would be highly micro-managed. Mind you I had not searched for the position. I was asked to apply based on my work ethic, background, and references from others in the company.

I was offered more money than I had ever made, but less than the current person holding the position. I could argue racism and sexism but that's another story for another day. Let's think back to Tamar, she had two husbands picked for her that were supposed to love and honor her but did not. They both passed away, due to not being who God needed them to be. I can imagine her feeling worthless as if something was wrong with her. Tamar was then promised the last son, but even that fell through. Many times in our lives we are tested, but we have to remember that, "For no matter how many promises God has made, they are Yes in Christ. And so through him, the Amen is spoken by us to the glory of God." 2 Corinthians 1:20. To me, this scripture is saying God's promises are yes and amen.

My mentor and I had a conversation where she reminded me of my worth and not to settle for less than I was worth. I am a highly educated woman with a degree and experience, and I came highly recommended. We discussed the pros and cons of taking the position. If I took this position as a single mom, and at the pay rate offered, I would be taking a great amount of time away from my young son. The increase in pay would cause other income issues such as an increase in child care and higher taxes. I prayed on it and God reminded me "For God is not a God of disorder but of peace as in all the congregations of the Lord's people." 1 Corinthians 14:33 To me, if this job was to be mine it would align with my beliefs, needs, and wants. I sent in my final offer and request. When they refused my counter offer without any negotiation, I had to walk away remembering the God that I serve does not make mistakes. What they did not know is that I had a not-for-profit ordained by God. I was instructed by God to take a layoff months later and to work the nonprofit full time. I now have many streams of income that I make on my terms that align with my beliefs, wants, and needs.

God loved Tamar so much that he did not forget about her or his promise in her life. She received not one but two heirs that were from the Father. Tamar did not have to settle for less. will come through and he has not forgotten about you. We go through times that we do not understand and it makes us wonder if our current situation is permanent. Remember trouble does not last always and joy will come in the morning.

She was not left to suffer in her brokenness. Tamar did not receive her promise in her time or when she wanted but it was right on time. Just as Jesus did not forget about me. I had to move out of the way because God's will was more than I could have ever imagined. He has definitely blown my mind and continues to do so. I share this with you to remind you of God's promise in your life. His promises are yes and amen. The journey has not been easy but it has been worth it. Had I not been obedient and took that walk by faith, I would not be receiving the fruits of my labor from what I call God's business. Business in which I am able to truly help others and minister to their hearts. Business where I am free to declare the power of his word daily.

Pray this prayer with me:
God thank You that my suffering won't last for long. The God of all grace, who called me to his eternal glory in Christ, after

I have suffered a little while, will himself restore me and make me strong, firm, and steadfast. (1 Peter 5:10). For I am your child and I shall fear not. Where I am weak you are strong. Where I fall short You show up and show out. Thank You, Father God, for never failing me and for guiding and teaching me. My failures are not my end, but a skill in learning to be the best me you have created me to be. With You all things are possible and nothing is impossible. Show me Your will and Your way father. With You, I will have the victory. This is my winning season! This is my winning season! This is my winning season! No matter how far the goals may seem, and no matter the number of times I might feel abandoned, I will overcome. I will succeed beyond what is imaginative father God in advance. Thank You! Amen.

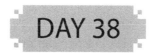

DAY 38

Be Unapologetically You
(Queen Vashti)
— Brittaney Pleasant —

"But when they conveyed the king's order to Queen Vashti, she refused to come. This made the king furious, and he burned with anger."
– Esther 1:12

THERE ARE MANY role models in the Bible. One of my favorites is Queen Vashti. She was very beautiful. One night her husband, King Xerxes, put on a banquet for the people in the fortress of Susa. Queen Vashti also put on a banquet for the women. After the king became drunk with wine, he summoned Queen Vashti to come and allow the men at his banquet to gaze upon her beauty. It is thought he requested that she come only wearing her royal crown. While others may have obeyed the king's order, Vashti refused to show herself and long story short, it cost her everything, including her position as Queen. This is so beautiful to me as it shows just how powerful Vashti was.

If you're wondering how she could be powerful when she lost it all, let me explain. Think about the world we live in today. Almost everywhere we turn there are women who are scantily dressed on television, in magazines, and on social media. If those same women refused to wear revealing clothing, most of them would probably be out of a job. I'm sure it took a lot of strength for Vashti to refuse to obey the king's commands, especially knowing what the consequences could be. I remember growing up and feeling as though I never fit in. This was especially true for high school when many of my friends were dressing "differently" to enhance and show off their newly developed curves. I must admit. I was not always as strong as Vashti. I wore short skirts and halter tops. I gave my body away seeking love and acceptance, only to end up feeling ashamed and even more disappointed with myself. Imagine if I would have had the courage that Vashti had to stand up and say, "This is who I am. This is what I stand for and I will not compromise my values for you, no matter who you may be."

I certainly learned the hard way, but you don't have to. Have you ever felt like this, Sis? If so, I want to let you know it's okay to start over again. Decide today that you are worth more. Decide that your self-respect is more important than popularity or attention. Know that you don't have to sacrifice your morals or values to win in life. God says you are already victorious. If this is something you are wrestling with, I want to encourage you to always be true to who you are. Stand up for your beliefs. Vashti understood the true meaning of being true to yourself and treating our body as a temple. Our bodies are sacred in the eyes of God and He desires that we honor Him by honoring ourselves. We don't know exactly what happened to Vashti after she was removed as queen. However, we do know that her courageous actions allowed her to leave with her dignity and self-respect and that is a truly beautiful thing.

Pray this prayer with me:

Dear Heavenly Father, I pray that You would help me to see that I do not have to use my beauty to gain the world and risk losing my soul. I pray that You would show me how to use my beauty for Your glory. Even if I have fallen short or compromised my values for others, remind me that I am forgiven by You and that Your mercies are new every day. In Jesus' name, I pray. Amen.

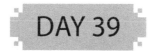
Don't Lose Confidence in God
(Widow of Zarephath)
— Shneice L. Hurd —

"For thus saith the Lord God of Israel, the barrel of meal shall not waste, neither shall the cruse of oil fail, until the day that the Lord sendeth rain upon the earth."
– 1Kings 17:14

IN THIS STORY of the widow of Zarephath, a woman and her son were down to their very last meal. The mother had already accepted defeat and planned to make one last meal for herself and her son, and die. A prophet came to her and asked if she could make a meal for him. She explained to him she had only enough for herself and her son. The prophet told her if she took the meal she had left and made it for him, the Lord of Israel would not allow her barrel of meal to run out. With nothing left to lose, the woman trusted what the prophet told her. She made a meal for him, and as promised, every time she went back to the barrel there was always enough for her to make another meal.

This story reminds me of the time I was pregnant with my oldest daughter. God kept me just like He did the woman in the story. Prior to my pregnancy with my oldest daughter, my husband and I experienced the loss of our first baby when I was almost 7 months pregnant. The devastation and heartbreak we felt was unexplainable. Without warning or any explanation from my doctor, the life we were expecting and planning for was over. During this time, I had not completely surrendered my life to God, and I did not know how to cope with the loss of my baby. However, this was my turning point, I knew nothing else could get me through the pain I was feeling, and I turned to God completely. I needed something no one else could give me. Not even alcohol or partying could touch the emptiness I was feeling.

About a year later I was pregnant again, and instantly I was overwhelmed with both excitement and fear. Although I had surrendered my life to Christ, I was still healing. During the pregnancy, I was put on bed rest and had to quit my job. I had to give myself shots in my stomach daily and was constantly in the ER. We were never given a reason as to why we lost our first child; we were just told: "these things happen". I was terrified but knew I had no other choice but to trust our Heavenly Father. Just as the woman chose to trust the Lord, so did I. The Bible says the Lord won't put more on us than we are able to bear. I knew I couldn't go through another loss so I held on to that scripture. I recall on my last visit to my high-risk doctor she told me I was going to lose this baby just like I lost my other baby. The comment devastated me but did not break my spirit.

Though at times it felt as if everything was against me, I in return immersed myself in the word of God and His promises. My oldest daughter will be 12 years old this year, and I give God all the glory! Sister, understand whatever trial you are going through is not too large for our Heavenly Father. One of my favorite phrases, "If He brings you to it, He will bring you through it!" Don't lose your confidence in the only one with the power to see you through!

Pray this prayer with me:

Father, in the name of Jesus, strengthen me for the journey You have set before me. In the word, You say that You will never leave nor forsake me, and if You are for me, You're more than the whole world against me. Right now, I am laying my trials at Your feet, and asking You to increase my confidence in You. I know You are with me, and I know that You are for me. Strengthen me for this season and give me peace that surpasses all understanding. In Jesus Name! Amen!

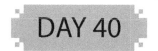

DAY 40

Always Trusting the Process
(Widow with Two Mites)
— Tiffany LaGrone —

And he looked up, and saw the rich men casting their gifts into
the treasury. And he saw also a certain poor widow casting in
thither two mites. And he said, Of a truth I say unto you, that this
widow hath cast in more than they all: For all these have of their
abundance cast in unto the offerings of God: but she of her penury
hath cast in all the living that she had.
– Luke 21: 1-4

STEPPING BACK AND taking a nice wide look at my life today in
comparison to the widow with the two mites, it's obvious that we
are parallel in various ways. Not knowing what the end result will be
I tend to waver in some decisions in life. Taking a leap of faith, I vow
to give Him all.

I recall years ago I fell on hard times. I was working a job that
didn't pay enough to take care of four children comfortably. I knew
that God would have to provide. Bills were piling up. The car note
was due. The rent was late. I felt I was slowly losing this battle. Until
one Sunday morning, I was sitting in church. I had only $30. Of
course, I thought about the food I would need to buy for the week,
enough to last us until I got paid again. I also knew I needed to put
gas in the car after service so I could get back and forth to work
for the rest of the week. As I sat there and they began to take up
an offering, God spoke to me. God said, "Give the entire $30 for the
offering." I was a little wary but I wanted to be obedient. I just had

one question for Him. I wanted to know if I would be ok. God spoke again and said, "Give all of it." When I got out of my seat to give the money, I felt a sense of relief.

Later that day I was invited to a family member's house for lunch right after church. I was really enjoying myself, eating, socializing, and just simply listening. Suddenly my cousin stood in front of everyone and called my name and handed me an envelope. I opened the envelope and there was three times the amount of money I had given for offering that Sunday. I was in disbelief. My heart started to smile. I was speechless. God had to remind me that obedience is better than sacrifice. It was a reminder that He is my provider. He is my Father. He loves me. He knows my needs. Proverbs 3:5 states "Trust in the LORD with all thine heart; and lean not unto thine own understanding.

So, all of this is a reminder that some things in life will not make sense to us but it's not up to us to understand. It is for us to trust and know that God has our best interests at heart. I feel He also wants to show His love for us in numerous ways. We have to recognize we need to take a step back and say, "Lord I trust You and I know You have a bigger and better plan for my life."

Pray this prayer with me:
Father God, I thank You for who You are. I ask, Father, that whoever is reading this will get a clear understanding of Your love for them. Your ways are not our ways and Your thoughts are not our thoughts, so I thank You that everything we sacrifice is for a greater purpose in Jesus Name. Amen.

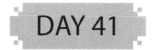
No Longer Thirsty!
(The Samaritan Woman at the Well)
— Rosie Thompson —

Jesus answered, "Everyone who drinks this water will be thirsty again, but whoever drinks the water I give them will never thirst. Indeed, the water I give them will become in them a spring of water welling up to eternal life."
– John 4:13-14

THE SAMARITAN WOMAN at the well lived a life of sin. She hadn't realized she needed a savior nor was she looking for one. But she had a thirst that she could not fill. She tried filling this thirst with different husbands. She had five and she wasn't even married to the man with whom she was currently living when she encountered Jesus at the well. Isn't that what many of us do? Looking for love in all the wrong places, trying to fill a void.

On this day she went to a well looking for water to quench her thirst. What she found was a man waiting. Was he waiting for a drink of water or her? The bible doesn't explicitly say but there he was upon her arrival. Jesus asked her for a drink of water. She almost dismissed him saying, "You are a Jew, and I am a Samaritan woman. Why are you asking me for a drink?" John 4:9

How many times have we dismissed the blessings of God because it didn't look like what we thought it should? If you're like me, you might have even said to God, "why are you asking me?" Why are you asking me to raise these children? Why are you asking me to build this business? Why are you asking me to pray for my husband? Why are you asking me to start this ministry? And God responds to us in a similar way that Jesus responds to this woman at the well saying, "If you only knew the gift God has for you..." He went on to say the gift he had for her was living water that if she drank it, she would never thirst again. And she did what a lot of us do, presented her doubt in the form of questions; asking God just how He was planning to accomplish this promise.

She said, "Sir, please give me this water!" Or in other words, "ok, I'll bite!" or "I'll try it. I'll do what you say but I'm still not sure about this." And Jesus proceeds to pour into her spiritual jug by telling her what He discerned about her life. He went on to explain that the time had come for people to worship God in spirit and in truth. And then the real truth bomb. He says to her, "I am the Messiah!" John 4:26 His response was so moving that she, "left her water jar beside the well and ran back to the village, telling everyone, 'Come and see a man who told me everything I ever did! Could he possibly be the Messiah?'"

I remember when I was searching for something and I didn't even know it. I tried different relationships, looking for love and acceptance. Nothing I did quenched the thirst that plagued my soul. I was never satisfied. I tried drinking, but I couldn't get drunk. I tried marijuana, but sleepy instead of high. I got tired of men really fast and would break up with them because the relationship wasn't fulfilling for me. I didn't know what was wrong with me. I just knew I didn't want to feel this way anymore. And one day, like the Samaritan woman, Jesus drew me to His well of living water. Hallelujah! I found out He was there all the time waiting on me. I discovered that I could never be satisfied because the thirst inside of me could only be filled by Jesus Christ! I was filled with the overflowing, living water of peace and joy! For the first time in my life, I was satisfied!

My thirst had been quenched. Oh, what a day that was! And just like the Samaritan woman I had to go and tell somebody that I had found a man, and this time, it was the right Man! I encourage you to partake of Jesus, that satisfying portion, so you never thirst again.

Pray this Prayer with Me:
Father, I found out I wasn't waiting on You, but You were waiting on me, and You did not fail me. You said in your word in John 4:14, "that whosoever drinks the water I give them will never thirst again." Well, here am I God saying fill me up until I thirst no more! I thank you, Father, that it is already done! In Jesus name amen! And it is so.

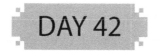

DAY 42

I Am Not My Past!
(A Woman Caught in Adultery)
— Jessica Jená Green —

Then Jesus stood up again and said to the woman, "Where are your
accusers? Didn't even one of them condemn you?" "No one, Lord,"
she answered. "Neither do I condemn you," said Jesus.
"Go, and from now on do not sin anymore."
– John 8:10-11

THERE ARE SO many women who aren't walking in their God-given
purpose because they don't feel worthy enough due to their past
mistakes and poor decisions. They are afraid that other people will
hold their past actions and behaviors against them. This fear holds
them in bondage.

The name of the woman whose story is told in John 8 isn't
given but her story is very significant and relatable. In this story, a
group of scribes and Pharisees confront Jesus while he is teaching
a session. They wanted Jesus to punish this woman who had been
caught in the act of adultery. The group of men made the woman
stand in the center of the crowd in hopes that Jesus would punish
her. They wanted to remind Jesus that according to the law of Moses
that the woman should be stoned to death. I believe that they not
only wanted the woman to be punished but they wanted her to be
humiliated.

Jesus shocked everyone when he bent down and began to
write on the ground with his finger. The bible doesn't say exactly
what Jesus was writing. However, some bible scholars believe that

Jesus was writing the names of the Pharisees, and the sins that they had committed. Others believe that he was writing down the ten commandments. Either way, whatever Jesus was writing humbled them severely.

The passage also tells us what Jesus said in between his writing. "The one without sin among you should be the first to throw a stone at her."John 8:7 This is a sweet reminder that no one can hold our sins against us. We also learn that as Jesus was writing on the ground the people accusing and condemning this woman began to leave one by one. Jesus then straightened up and asked the woman where her accusers were and after realizing that they had all disappeared Jesus told her to leave and sin no more.

A lot of times we allow people to hold our past mistakes and poor decisions against us, including ourselves. But today I want you to remember that God doesn't call you by your sin, your insecurities, your mistakes, your poor decisions, or what the world may call you. He calls you daughter. God calls you blessed, forgiven, chosen, free, and wonderfully made. Don't let life make you lose grip on God's word over your life. Today, stop holding your past against you! Stop holding the things you did when you didn't know who you were, against yourself. Holding on to who you were or to what you have done, won't change the past. I challenge you, Sis, to allow your past to position you for your purpose. Sis, allow your pain to empower your purpose! "You intended to harm me, but God intended it all for good." Genesis 50:20

Pray this prayer with me:

Daddy, I pray that I stop allowing others and myself to hold my past against me. Thank you that was intended to harm me, is being used for my good! Your word says that if I am in Christ, then I am a new creature. God, I choose to walk boldly and confidently in the newness that you offer in Jesus name. I pray to receive the power to understand how wide, how long, how high, and how deep your love for me is God. Lord, I want to experience the love of Christ, even though it is too great to understand fully. By understanding your unfailing love, I will be made complete with all the fullness of life and the power that comes from you Lord. (Ephesians 3:18-19). I declare and decree that I am not my past but that I am free, forgiven, and loved by God and that my future is bright. In Jesus' name, I pray. Amen.

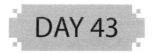

DAY 43

You Are Deserving of God's Love
(Woman with the Alabaster Jar)
— Shneice L. Hurd —

"Wherefore I say unto thee, Her sins, which are many are forgiven; for she loved much: but to whom little is forgiven, the same loveth little."
– Luke 7:47

IN THIS STORY, Jesus was eating a meal with the Pharisees when a woman came in with her alabaster jar. In reverence, she broke open the jar and poured it out on Jesus' feet as He sat in awe of her actions. She began to cover His feet with kisses. As she cried, drenching His feet with her tears she dried them with her hair. The woman did not have the best reputation, but her reputation could not stop her from emptying her heart out to Jesus. The Pharisees talked about her and expressed their disapproval of her presence and actions. She could have allowed the thoughts of others, and her indiscretions, to keep her hiding in a bubble of shame, but she didn't! On this day she boldly came to Jesus and offered to Him the very thing that represented her. Just as Jesus did not turn the woman away, He will not turn you away. He did not ask her for an explanation or rebuke her for the sins she had committed. He simply said, "Her sins, which are many are forgiven." Understand, my sister, God is not like man!

In the story, I saw my old self from 13 years ago, at the start of my journey with Christ. Very much like the woman in the story I was full of sin, shame, and extreme brokenness. I was a young lady who knew the life I was living was completely opposite to what was acceptable in God's eyes. I was damaged and blinded by all the drinking, partying, and promiscuous behavior. I was used to soothing my pain, hurt, fear, and discomfort with whatever came to mind. Although I knew the comfort was temporary, I told myself a quick fix was good enough.

I was afraid to go to God with my emotional struggles. I felt I was supposed to have myself presentable, spiritually, before He would accept me. Ultimately, I did not want to let God down. I thought there was a checklist I had to pass to make myself worthy and deserving of God's time and love. I recall the many times I would go to church wanting God to help me but feared disappointing Him. I would go back a few months later needing God to see me but embarrassed about what others might be thinking of me. Then I recall going to church one Sunday and hearing the late Pastor Sammie LaGrone preaching agape love. He described this love as the highest form of love, also known as unconditional love. He explained that agape love was the kind of love our Heavenly Father has for all His children; for everyone.

That day I begin to realize God did not view me the way others did, and not even the way I viewed myself. Looking back at the story as the woman was crying at the feet of Jesus, I believe she was utterly consumed and overwhelmed by His complete acceptance of her. Wow! This story cancels out any negative notion that anyone could ever tell you about what God thinks of you. He is not asking you to prove yourself; He is not even asking you to fix yourself. He is simply saying come as you are My daughter; come to Me and I will give you rest. He loves us simply because He knows exactly who He has created us to be. He is not moved by our failures, nor is He angered by our imperfections. It wasn't until I fell at the feet of Jesus that I began to sincerely feel loved and accepted. No, everything was not perfect from the second I chose Jesus, but I can honestly say my life has been an uphill journey since. I'm a much stronger woman, mother, and wife, and I give Him all the glory.

When you are going through an extremely difficult moment and you hear a voice telling you God can't love someone like you, remember God is not surprised by your mess-ups. He's sitting and waiting for you to give your heart to Him because, unlike man, God's love is truly without conditions. I'm married to my high school crush going on 13 years this year, and even the love that we have for one another does not compare to the love I've encountered with God. Surrendering my heart to God was by far the BEST decision I've made in my life. Don't allow fear to keep you from the only one who is capable of loving you the way you deserve. Sister, allow Him to heal you, nurture you, strengthen you, and reestablish you. Isaiah 61:7 "Instead of your shame there shall be a double portion; instead of dishonor they shall rejoice in their lot; therefore, in their land, they shall possess a double portion; they shall have everlasting joy."

Father, in the name of Jesus, from today forward I pray that You give me Your eyes to see me as You see me. I will not allow my imperfections to dictate the woman of God You have created me to be. I will seek Your comfort and love anytime I'm feeling at my lowest, and I will not allow what others say to make me forget what You say about me. I am fearfully and wonderfully made; created in Your image, and for Your glory. Before I was formed in my mother's womb You knew me, and before I was born You set me apart. I now know I have purpose. I know I'm worthy to be loved, and today I surrender my heart to You, Lord. In Jesus Name. Amen!

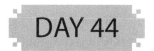

DAY 44

You Can't Stay Here, Sis
(Woman with the Issue of Blood)
— Allison Denise Arnett —

But Jesus turned and saw her. "Have courage, daughter," He said.
"Your faith has made you well." And the woman was made well
from that moment.
– Matthew 9:22 HSCB

I REMEMBER READING a young man's comment on social media once that said, "Never trust anything that bleeds for seven days and lives." I thought "Ouch, someone hurt him badly." Then later in life, I was introduced to a woman who bled for 12 years and yet still found the ability to trust God. 12 years of most likely not being able to have children or potentially a successful marriage because of her condition. 12 years of believing for but not receiving healing. Even after 12 years of not understanding why she was different from the other women around her, her hope for healing is still yet evident in the text. It said she "had spent all she had on doctors". No one spends all they have unless they believe their situation has even the slightest probability of improving.

I imagine her hearing about Jesus' approach and thinking to herself, "This is worth a try! If He is who He says He is and can do what they say he's done, then this is my chance!" We do not know if she was alone or not. We don't know if she was in physical pain or not. We only know that she had been in this place a long time, and probably from her point of view, way too long. We also know that she had pressed her way through crowds of people, some just being curious and others in need of their own healing. I feel her anticipation rising with each step towards Jesus; with each "pardon me" she breathed knowing that her life could be about to change forever.

Sis, sometimes all it takes is one moment with God to positively change the entire trajectory of your life. One night with the King. One touch of His garment. One miraculous conception. One heartfelt prayer. One divine appointment. One resolve to do it with God this time. In her one moment, she walked up behind Jesus in the midst of chaos and touched her one moment destined to change her life forever.

I've been there. A few short years ago, I found myself stuck in a cycle of looking for love everywhere except in God. He could have turned His back on me. He could have decided I was unfaithful and unworthy of His affection. He could have written me off and divorced me. What happened instead? God healed my heart. He looked upon me with love in His eyes and sincerity in His heart and said, "You are mine. I have called you by name. This world can't love you as I do." He said, "I know you don't understand a father's love because the Dad I gave you couldn't show you. I know you don't understand the commitment required for a successful marriage which is why you are twice divorced. I know it is hard to understand that I will never abandon you as countless others have. But I am here. Forever committed to you." God started working things out in my soul. He did not leave me in my traumatized state.

He couldn't leave her in the same condition either. Look at the heart of God for her, this woman who we know by condition and not by name. God loved her so much that He would not leave her where she had been those last 12 years. The moment she touched Him, the moment she activated her faith in Him, He brought her out. You see, it's one thing to believe a thing. It's a whole other ball game to act on that belief. And so, my questions to you today are, do you believe you can come out of that thing? And what are you going to do about it? I challenge you to activate your faith in God today.

> **Pray this prayer with me:**
> Father, I am ready for my "one moment" with You. I am ready to come out of this thing. It's been too long. Lord, I open my heart for You to come in and mend the broken pieces of my heart and reveal just how deep You love me. Lord, I thank You that You never leave me nor forsake me. That I can have courage because my faith in You is making me whole. I want what You want for me. I know it is Your desire for me to dwell in love, joy, peace, patience, kindness, goodness, faithfulness, gentleness, and self-control. Deliver me! Restore me, oh Lord! In Jesus' name. Amen. And it is so!

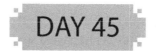

DAY 45

Your Sacrifice is Not in Vain
(Woman Whose Baby Was Stolen in the Night)
— Shneice L. Hurd —

"Everyone in Israel was amazed when they heard how Solomon
had made his decision. They realized that God had given him
wisdom to judge fairly."
– 1Kings 3:28

IN THIS STORY two women had babies, but the baby of one of the
women died during the night. The woman whose baby died switched
babies with the women whose baby was alive. The woman whose
baby was stolen woke up and noticed the dead baby lying next to
her was not her baby. She knew the other woman had switched
babies with her. In an effort to have this crime settled they brought
the matter before King Solomon. He listened to both sides and, then
offered them a very extreme solution. He recommended the baby
who was alive be cut in half and split between the two women. The
woman whose baby was really dead agreed to his decision. The real
mother pled with King Solomon to not harm her baby but instead
allow the other woman to keep it. The sacrifice she was willing to
make was the proof Solomon needed to determine who the real
mother was, and then he declared that the baby be given to the
woman who interceded for her child's life to be spared.

This story reminds me of my walk with Christ in my marriage.
Much like the mother in the story I found out when I began to
sacrifice my will to God's will, He moved faster on my behalf. In
the beginning of my marriage, we went through some growing

pains and they were indeed painful. I was 22 years old and knew absolutely nothing about how to have a successful godly marriage. After an entire one week of marriage (yes, I said one week) I was ready to call it quits. I thought I had made the biggest mistake of my life. We were merely two kids trying to figure things out. I wanted things my way and he wanted things his way. Over and over I would hear our pastor emphasize, Ephesians 6:12 "We wrestle not against flesh and blood, but against principalities, against powers, against the rulers of the darkness of this world, against spiritual wickedness in high places."

While I heard the scripture repeatedly it took me a while to grasp what it truly meant. I experienced an emotionally abusive relationship prior to my marriage so I was very defensive and afraid to let my guard down. It got to the point that I was completely drained. Everything I tried didn't work. Once I realized I was fighting a spiritual battle in the flesh I then gave my entire marriage to God. I stopped focusing on who was right and wrong and begin to examine my own self and surrendered my feelings, pride, self-pity, and need to be understood to God. Understand, sister, God is sovereign. Nothing we come across in this walk with Him is out of His control. Once I was willing to sacrifice my will for His I saw a major turn-around in my home. We went from arguing daily to laughing daily, and I give all honor and glory to God. It's okay to lose yourself in God. It's not until you lose yourself in Him that you learn who you truly are. He has proven to me that when I exchange my will for His will, He will restore everything, and when He restores... HE RESTORES.

Pray this prayer with me:

Father, in the name of Jesus, help me to understand that You can and will turn all things around for the good for those who love You and are called according to Your purpose. Help me to learn that when I feel like I can't trust anyone else I can trust You. Teach me to lean not to my own understanding. I know You are for me, and I give You permission to have Your way in me today. In Jesus name. Amen!

MEET THE AUTHORS

ALLISON DENISE

ALLISON DENISE IS a 7x Best Selling Author, International Speaker, and Award-Winning Graphic Designer of beautiful boss brands and books through her biz Brand It Beautifully™. A servant leader at heart and an eclectic, creative soul, she seeks to help others free their creativity while transforming lives. An avid advocate of Self-Acceptance and Spiritual Empowerment it is her desire that every woman finds the power in their voice and the beauty in their story. She did not know that her love for God and building others up would lead to success in the marketplace and in ministry. This book collaboration is her vision from God to merge all of her loves into one. She prays that something you experience, someone you meet, or something you do as a result of this book will ignite the fire in you to Empower Your Inner Creator™ and become everything God designed you to be.

Connect on Instagram and Facebook @ImAllisonDenise
On the Web www.AllisonDeniseMinistries.com
Podcast: EmpowerYourInnerCreator.com also available on Spotify and Apple Podcasts

BREJETTE N. TERRY-EMERY

BREJETTE N. TERRY-EMERY is the Co-Founder of the nonprofit Inspirempower New Mexico and Executive Director of the local Dress for Success Albuquerque an affiliate of the worldwide Dress for Success organization. Prior to this role, Brejette served the community in several positions case management, career transition specialist, and community outreach specialist for 8 years. During this time Brejette gained skills by providing guidance, mentoring, and career pathways for Albuquerque's at-risk youth and their families. Brejette holds a Bachelor of Science in Family Studies/ Human Development and Family Relations and also a Minor in Africana Studies from the University of New Mexico. Brejette splits her time pursuing a career in motivational speaking, inspirational and empowerment coaching and most importantly raising her amazingly, bright son.

BRITTANEY PLEASANT

BRITTANEY PLEASANT IS first a wife, mother, and child of God. Like many women today, she wears many different hats. In addition to her duties at home, Brittaney is the founder of Be H.E.R., a transformational speaker, author, and mentor. As The Marital Strategist, she helps wives and those on the journey to becoming wives who are struggling with intimacy due to reproductive health challenges and emotional trauma. She is known for her compassion, determination, and dedication to helping women overcome and use the struggles and obstacles of their past to live fulfilling lives. Brittaney speaks from her experiences and is passionate about teaching women how to use the Word of God as their foundation and guide in life. She believes that by teaching women how to live according to Biblical standards, women everywhere will experience a supernatural shift in every area of their lives.

CLARICE CREGGER

CLARICE IS A creative entrepreneur specializing in life coaching and professional photography. As a certified life coach, she specializes in transformational coaching with a keen focus on breaking harmful patterns and overcoming guilt and shame. With a compelling backstory of her own, Clarice is very passionate about helping women find their voice, strength, and beauty while overcoming past hurts. With a backdrop of faith in God, Clarice helps women and anyone in need fulfil their God-given purpose in life.

Clarice founded BBBM March 2019, God has had this mission in her heart for 2 years. She created BBBM as a platform that allows women to speak, share, and see that she is not alone! Clarice has overcome many trials and tribulations in her life that allows her to relate with other women and to testify how God saved her every single time...Her mantra? "I help you release, reflect, refocus, and restart — Are you ready?"

CLARISSA PRITCHETT, M.P.H

CLARISSA PRITCHETT, M.P.H, is an Integrative Nutrition Health and Life Coach, Speaker, Author, Entrepreneur, and Army Medical Service Corps Officer. Clarissa is a wife and mom to 3 beautiful boys. Clarissa is passionate about health and wellness and has served numerous clients over the past 18 years in health and fitness. She has a B.S. in Health Education and M.P.H. in Nutrition. She is the founder of Healthy Family Kitchen and provides women/families with nutrition programs and strong faith-fueled life recipes for life. Clarissa is also the founder of Empire Posh Queens and mentors young women to start home businesses while promoting Sisterhood, Self-Care, and Service to those in need. She loves to encircle and uplift women to live healthy lives. She is a sought-out Speaker and Resilience Instructor for the military, wellness companies, and local churches to share her story and to motivate women with their health and life goals. Clarissa is a short, sweet, and spicy mixed salad sistah that keeps it real, raw, and organic about how she overcame many health challenges and body issues with God's love. Overall, her favorite things in life are Jesus, family, friends, cooking, and eating food, especially tacos, chocolate, and donuts with sprinkles!

DEBORAH RIVERS DECOTEAU

DEBORAH RIVERS DECOTEAU is a Best Selling Author, Wellness Director, and Caribbean Carnival Costume Designer and Band Leader. A native of Trinidad and Tobago she has dedicated her life to bringing awareness to her culture via singing, dancing, and writing. It is her life's work to empower women to wellness and to live a life by God's design. Deborah is a mother of five and is affectionately known by her grandchildren as Little G. When she is not adding building blocks to her legacy, you will find her in Houston, Texas crafting to keep her creative ideas flowing.

JESSICA JENA GREEN

JESSICA GREEN BETTER known as Jessica Jená is an Educator, host of the "Released Women" Podcast, Author, and the founder of the Released Women Community. Jessica believes that her purpose is to bring good news to the poor, to bind up the brokenhearted, to proclaim release for captives and liberation for prisoners. To give a crown in place of ashes, oil of joy in place of mourning, and a mantle of praise in place of discouragement. (Isaiah 61:1-3) She strives to help women looking to go to the next level with their self-esteem, purpose, and their walk with God. She is passionate about cultivating the confidence within others so that they may walk boldly and freely in everything God has predestined for them. Jessica uses faith, transparency, and her own experiences to help the women God has assigned to her voice.

MONIQUE M. MOORER

MONIQUE M. MOORER is a servant of God, wife, and mother of three. As a nurse for over twenty-one years, she has served her community in multiple states. Monique has even become a keynote speaker talking to young girls and their parents about changes to their bodies during puberty. As a minister of the gospel, she has served the church in multiple capacities including praise and worship leader. Monique is an encourager at heart. Her lively and vibrant personality can uplift almost any room. Although Monique has encountered moments of hardship and despair, she will not allow those situations to tarnish her view of her Savior. She is confident in her relationship with God which keeps her pressing forward. While embarking on this devotional journey discover how God can use you too, as we are all living testimonies. Monique wants to remind you that often we do not see it, but just like her, God has a specific plan and purpose with you in mind that will blow your mind.

NATALIE BRYAN, LCSW

NATALIE BRYAN, LCSW is a three-time best-selling author that has been devoted to serving her community and advocating for others. After completing her B.S. in Interdisciplinary Studies with a focus in Early Childhood and Psychology, Natalie went on to complete her Master's in Social Work at Adelphi University. Natalie has worked in the health and human services field for over 15 years which includes experience in case management, child protective services, mental health clinical services, and working with our veterans. Natalie is the owner of Restoring Harmony Counseling and Consulting, and she is also the founder of P.E.A.R.L, an organization that focuses on children and families in our community. The acronym stands for Providing Education and Advocacy to Rebuild lives.

PATTI DENISE HENRY

A NATIVE OF the Island of Trinidad & Tobago, Patti is internationally recognized as a Minister, Psalmist, Teacher, Hospice Chaplain, Family & Bereavement Counselor, Best Selling Author, and Prolific Speaker. She is also known as "A Prophetic Worshiper" as her sound in the earth impacts the heart and mind of all who come into contact with her ministry.

Patti Henry uses Biblical insight along with life experiences to help you to identify "The Holes in Your Soul" and provide the necessary tools to transform you into "Beautiful Souls".

She is the Founder & President of Patti Denise International Ministries, The Soul Coach, and Sisters, Let's Keep Talking! Patti is humbled by the call that God has placed on her life and is very passionate about her purpose which is to multiply disciples for Christ and to function as a Soul Coach where she motivates others to live before they die. She is indeed a Servant Leader for such a time as this.

ROBIN CUFFEE-KING

ROBIN CUFFEE-KING IS a delegation professional who has made it her mission to brighten, nurture, and heal God's people. Robin is a gentle spirit who works hand in hand in her community to help enrich the lives of others. Robin also has a passion and zeal to see business professionals succeed in their industry so she works diligently to build collaborations and to educate other professionals on successful delegation strategy. Robin is a wife, mother, among many other things but feels most accomplished in being a woman of God.

ROSIE THOMPSON

ROSIE THOMPSON IS a devoted wife, mother, grandmother, and minister of the Gospel of Jesus Christ. She has a deep desire to ensure she has a strong, ongoing relationship with her Heavenly Father. In her local church, she serves on the board, leads praise and worship, and leads engaging bible study small groups. She has a heart for people and transparently shares with others her life's journey as a testimony of God's goodness. When she is not writing you can find her fulfilling her deepest passion of doing community outreach for the church.

SHNEICE HURD

SHNEICE HURD IS a devoted wife and stay-at-home mother of three and is on the most significant journey of her life as an active youth minister at her church. With a passion to impact those around her, she has a desire to start an organization for young adults and kids who are struggling with who they are in Christ. Her passion is to show the unconditional love of Christ to everyone she meets. She is an encourager at heart and a realist by habit. A simple woman of God, willing vessel by choice, saved by grace and chosen by God.

TIFFANY LAGRONE

TIFFANY LAGRONE IS a single mother of four, an entrepreneur in her heart. She is the creator and the founder of Tiffany's Unlimited Hair Design and the future Christ-Like Learning Center. A youth leader at Jesus Tabernacle Church an ordained youth minister, and a lover of souls. She delights herself in serving others with love and compassion. She seeks after God's heart while creating an atmosphere of joy and peace.

She was a woman that didn't know her worth until God spoke to her in the year 2000. Realizing she needed a change, she developed a closer relationship with God. Although the battle was great and the trails continued, she realized that she had to put her complete trust in God. Not knowing what would result in letting her child go, she knew she had to make a decision to weather the storm.

After years of fighting and warring with the enemy, she always came out victorious. Now recognizing God's plan and purpose for her life, she has chosen to give up everything that will hinder her from her calling. Letting go of all hurt and pain, forgiving others for what was done to her. She chose to surrender all to God in her most desperate times. While raising her children in the fear of Lord, she decided to let them go at a certain age so they could thrive, and so she could deepen her personal relationship with God. She continues to leap over walls, kick down doors while looking to Him for everything. She still is and always remains a conqueror. For many years she has stood and continues to stand on God's uncompromising word. She communicates with Him daily. She seeks after His will and nothing else. "WHO IS SHE?", you may ask. She is powerful, mighty, and triumphant.

VICKEY NEAL

Vickey Neal is an inspiring woman of God. She is seeking to impact the world through the word of God while being led by the Spirit. The life that she lived before receiving Christ as her Lord and Savior is an amazing testimony of God's love. To this day she seeks His face out of the gratefulness of her heart understanding that in everything God led her to that He was also there to bring her through it. The strength that she had to live and not die was gain, and that which she seeks to gain is to touch the lives of many souls and to let them know that God is not a man that he should lie (Numbers 23:19). It has been 28 years since she has given her life totally to Christ. She is now living a journey of God's unfailing love.